EMANUEL
& ME

Emanuel & Me

Copyright © Jac Turner 2022

All rights reserved. No part of this book may be reproduced in any form, including photocopying and recording, without permission in writing from the publisher, except for brief quotes in review or reference.

The book information is catalogued as follows;
Author Name(s): Jac Turner
Title: Emanuel & Me
Description; First Edition

Book Design by Lynda Mangoro

ISBN (paperback) : 978-1-914447-41-9
ISBN (ebook) : 978-1-914447-42-6

Prepared by That Guy's House Ltd.
www.ThatGuysHouse.com

EMANUEL
& ME

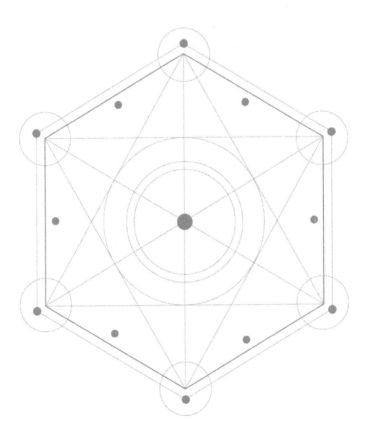

JAC TURNER

I dedicate this book to
Jason, Katie, Euan & Eva
who lovingly support me in everything I do.

Contents

Welcome to Emanuel & Me... 9

Chapter One: Who are you? 13

Chapter Two: Why are you here? 29

Chapter Three: : What do you want to say in your book Emanuel? 41

Chapter Four: Humanity & Clarity 57

Chapter Five: Let go, surrender, be free, be happy 71

Chapter Six: Learn to Listen 83

Chapter Seven: Past Lives and Insights 101

Chapter Eight: Spiritual Awakening 115

Chapter Nine: Our Soul Plan 131

Chapter Ten: So, what happens now, Emanuel? 147

Final Word From Me 159

Welcome to Emanuel & Me...

I have been guided throughout my life's journey surrounded by Spirit, even when I didn't even know this was possible. From a young age, I felt the calling of something more and heard the whispers of words from those I could not see.

In this book, I refer to *angels*, *Spirit* and *God*. To explain my reference point of God, I believe it to be our higher and supreme being – the creator of all things. *Angels and spirit guides* (or divine helpers) are intermediaries between God and human beings, or so I believe. They are our messengers and are here to teach us grace, bring us laughter, and help us find our higher calling in this lifetime.

Connecting and working with our divine helpers is something that we are all capable of, and I will be sharing ways for you to begin your own communication journey with them so you can learn to trust your own inner knowledge and receive clarity for the highest growth of your soul.

In this book, we will go on a journey of eternal wisdom with channelled guidance from my spirit guide, *Emanuel*. I once would have never imagined it possible to receive information directly from Spirit. But with loving messages channelled from Emanuel and gladly received with love, I discovered my purpose: sharing guidance and infinite words of wisdom that have travelled through thousands of years and still resonate with us today.

I was born a wee Scottish lassie and brought up in Glasgow. Neither of my parents were very religious, but thankfully, my grandmother and her sisters were very spiritual. One of my grandaunts was particularly connected with the Spiritualist Church (which would have been very woo woo at the time). I have often wished I could have a conversation with her now, to see what sort of seances and tea leaf readings they got up to.

By the time I was a teenager, my spiritual encounters were pretty much a daily occurrence. I would see people and feel them trying to talk to me and would especially hear my name being called very clearly.

As I had absolutely no understanding of what was going on, and this being something that I couldn't bring up for discussion at the dinner table, I soon became fearful of this communication from the unknown. With fear fuelling my power of intention, I seemed to be able to switch it off, avoid it and pretend that it wasn't even there.

I managed with this for a while, although I always found myself drawn to books about dream meanings, palmistry, astral travel, or angels. I now recognise this as Spirit's way of trying to catch my attention, despite my efforts to shut off.

In my 20s, I trained as a beauty therapist, a career that I loved. This led me on a journey of connecting with other therapists and therapies. I soon found myself led onto the lightworkers' path by being introduced to Reiki and later becoming a Reiki Master, Crystal Healer and Angel Healing Practitioner. Furthermore, in recent years I found my way to the Spiritualist Church where I was introduced to mediumship for self-acceptance, growth and spiritual development.

Over the years, I have had many encounters with Spirit, such as Mr. Baxter, a man who used to live in our current home for 17 years prior to his passing. Mr. Baxter, it seemed, liked to listen to the radio at lunchtime, as every day around 12pm he would step into the kitchen and turn our radio on. This was his way of letting me know that he was still around and was interested in seeing what was going on. His spirit only stayed around for a few weeks after we moved in and left us once we had fully settled in. I believe he was happy to move on with the knowledge that his home was being looked after.

Connecting with our loved ones in Spirit through mediumship is something that I have learned to do, but this isn't the only type of communication with spirit guides. I have received and written many messages through the art of channelling, and this book is both the story and wisdom from my greatest spiritual encounter yet: Emanuel, hence the title, *Emanuel & Me*.

All the pathways of my life have now led me to this moment, to sharing this book with you.

As I invite you into the journey of *Emanuel & Me*, we will share our spiritual connection through our past life interrelation and discover why he has chosen to communicate through me in this current time. We will explore Emanuel's timeless wisdom for inner light, knowledge, and self-discovery. We will also study the different stages of spiritual awakening and spiritual laws and discover an entire universe of methods that will guide you in connecting with your own spirit guides.

It is my hope that this book will bring faith, hope, and clarity to all that are ready to receive it.

Let's begin ...

CHAPTER ONE

WHO ARE YOU?

When I am ready or feel drawn to connect to Emanuel, I usually go sit on my bed and make myself comfortable, with a little notebook and pen to hand. I take a moment to relax and close my eyes whilst I say a little prayer and invite him forward to connect with me. As he steps forward, I feel the shift in energy around me. It usually makes me smile, as I know then that we are ready to begin ...

Are you my guardian angel?

No.

Are you an angel?

No.

Are you my spirit guide?

Yes, we were connected before your birth into this lifetime, child.

We have been on many journeys together; I am your trusted friend.

We have lived and fought battles together.

We will again re-unite in time.

It has been a long journey to get you to this point, but I am glad that you are here.

I started writing with Spirit way back in 2004 after I had attended a book signing event at my local bookstore with the author Trudy Griswald. She was hosting an informational talk on her book at the time, *Angel Speak*. The event was a part of her book launch campaign and the topic was 'How to Connect and Write with Your Angels'.

Watching and listening to Trudy speak so passionately and inspirationally about the ability to connect and write with angels resonated with me on a deeper level. It struck a chord in me with a feeling that I just could not explain, and I wanted to know more. So, being totally in love with this idea of being able to connect with the angels, I purchased a copy of the book and had it signed on the inside cover by Trudy herself, with a little note that said, 'Your angels want to speak to you.' Little did I know then that this was to become my reality.

I read the book from cover to cover. I found the writing so clear and easy to follow, with step-by-step instructions on how to bring the teaching words from the divine into your heart and everyday life. And I wanted this so much to be true for my own life at the time. I set out to get my own little journal for writing in, and it all started from there.

On the opening page of my journal, I proudly set out the following prayer. I have always believed that prayer is a positive way to set the intention for good and a way to invite the connection between worlds. To this day, I still repeat this prayer before asking for any guidance:

Angel of God, my guardian dear

To whom God's love commits me here

Ever this day be at my side

To light and love

To rule and guide

Thank you

Amen.

On the next page of my journal, I followed the instructions from the book, which said, 'Just ask.' I didn't actually know what to ask, so the first words that I wrote were, 'Are you there?' I waited for a reply, but nothing happened.

So, I went on to writing, 'Do you hear me?' And still nothing happened.

This went on for a few weeks, to be honest; I wrote a question and waited for an answer. Sometimes I would even sit and stare at my pen, wondering why it hadn't written anything. Like it was the pen's fault! But I was not going to be put off or defeated, even though I did feel a little deflated at times and was beginning to think the technique was a load of old rubbish.

I even spent time wondering what I had done wrong, questioning myself and thinking that maybe I wasn't good enough. I second-guessed myself, wondering if I actually believed in this form of communication, or even thinking that the angels didn't really want to talk to me, or maybe I just didn't know how to ask the right questions. The inner self really does everything it can to talk you out of believing anything is possible at times. In reflection, it took a little bit of time, patience, and persistence to get things going.

Firstly, I realised that I needed to set myself some quiet time regularly to sit with my journal ready to write my answers from Spirit. And secondly, I needed to ask some questions.

Do you hear me?

Can you hear me?

Does this actually work?

These were some of my very first questions that I asked.

Over time, I worked out that all I needed to do was relax, trust in the process, and spend less time beating myself up through trying to force an answer to happen. It was only then, during this moment of self-realization, that I had a truly overwhelming feeling of love. It felt like being wrapped up in cottonwool, my head was all light and fuzzy, and I had an inner knowing of the words to write on my paper. *Trust!!* would be my first written word from Spirit.

As you can imagine, my reaction was, 'WOW, this actually does work!' followed by the excitement of 'What will I do next?' This lift in vibration left a zest for more and encouraged me to keep on going with the momentum. Over time, my one written word on a page expanded into one sentence across the page, then into a paragraph which eventually extended to a full message of inspirational writing across a full A4 page.

I mention this to let you know that patience is the key when connecting with the divine; you will never be given something that you are not ready to receive.

When I started asking for my own guidance in this way, I always received the words of support that I was looking for.

In a way, it was a bit like working with oracle cards. I would ask a question and feel drawn to the answer, only in this instance, I would feel drawn to write the answer, rather than pulling a card.

Looking back, I had no idea of the importance of the job I had to do here, or the importance of the words that I was receiving. I had been almost selfish with my writings as

I was only ever asking for myself, my own guidance, my own purpose, and I never shared any of the information with others. It was my own little sanctuary of peace.

It was many years later, after revisiting some of my own writings, that I found validation in the words. The guidance I had received was all appropriate to the time in question. I always tried to date the journal sessions, so I could keep track of the time scale in question. Many of my writings have given me clear and honest support through difficult times in my own personal life. I have laughed at some of the weird and wonderful questions I asked and also at the humour in some of the written replies. It was only on looking back at all these messages that I noticed they were all signed off in a similar way. At the end of each message, at the bottom of each page they were signed, 'Amen Emanuel'.

In this book, I am about to share with you the wonderful words of wisdom that have been shared with me, from Spirit, to bring light, hope and love into your world.

So, what exactly is a spirit guide?

This is a question that many will ask and there are many ways to answer this, but to keep it simple, your spirit guide is helping you along your life path, trying to guide you and steer you in the right direction of your life.

Sometimes for us, this is an easy quest and at other times, an impossible task. You will have many guides in many forms through your lifetime. But essentially, one spirit guide will be assigned to you, child, from the day of your birth until the day of your death or your ascension back to Spirit.

And even though we are here to guide you, in every possible way, you each of course have your own free will and are in total control of the decisions you make in everyday life. Steering away from your chosen path from time to time is also good learning, as this allows you to gain real life experience, which, after all, is what you are born onto the Earth to achieve.

As you are a spirit guide, have you walked the Earth?

Yes, indeed; this question makes me smile now, child. For it has taken many years to get you to this point, full of faith and trust in your heart; you are open to receive.

I have lived many lifetimes on Earth, child.

I was a warrior with you, a soldier of honour.

I am proud to be of your service, child, for your light of God shines bright within you.

Are you saying that we were soldiers together?

Yes, you walked by my side, my child, fully dressed with pride, ready for battle

We met as we were walking through Westerwood, or marching, I should I say.

We met under a star-filled night sky, glazed with hope.

As we walked with honour and patrolled the path beneath us, it brought us both pleasure and comfort in the stillness to follow.

Through research, I found that Westerwood was indeed a place where soldiers would have been present.

It is located in the Northeast of Cumbernauld in

North Lanarkshire, Scotland. Historically, it was the site of a Roman fort posted along the Antonine Wall. Its neighbouring forts were Croyhill to the west and Castlecary to the east. The Westerwood Fort was the fourth smallest known to be located along the wall.

The Antonine Wall was known to the Romans as Vallum Antonini. It was the Roman Empire's northwest frontier. The wall was the most inspiring building project that the people of Scotland would have seen in their time. It was constructed upon the orders of the Emperor Antonius Pius around the year 142 AD, some 20 years after Hadrian's Wall was built.

The wall would shine as a symbol of Rome's power and authority. It stretched for 37 miles across Scotland's central belt, covering areas from Bo'ness on the Firth of Forth to old Kilpatrick on the River Clyde and would have taken you 12 hours to walk it.

Of course, in Roman times, there was no such named country as Scotland. The area covered in the Latin Britannia, or Britain as we know it, was then called Caledonia.

What happened next?

We followed in the light of the stars

to a place of sanctuary

for this is where our journey begins.

By sanctuary, do you mean a church?

Yes, child, our altar for prayer, our temple.

Now listen, please.

In meeting, we were guided to our spiritual paths.

It was the opening of our hearts and minds.

We had a sense of belonging.

We were sent to God to pray.

We found comfort in our prayers

and a hope in the almighty.

To help me understand your words here, are you saying that we prayed for God's assistance to give us hope?

Yes, child.

Our prayers were received by God, and we were, furthermore, loved.

We shall succeed in this journey, just as we did then.

The almighty took great pleasure in assigning me to you, for years have passed since our first meeting when we vowed once again to become one.

Can you tell me more about Westerwood, please?

Yes, child, it was our home, our learning, our experience of life in both living and dying.

It gave us a sense of belonging, as there were many soldiers around us, for bonds were made of trust and honour here.

As we marched out along the path at night

where the stars were shining so bright,

peace and calm were all around us,

there was not a sound,

then the screams of battle began,

with bloodshed and tears surround.

We were guided by the light of God

to a safe place and waited for the sun again.

What were we fighting for?

Land, I believe. It was our job, our honour, our life.

We trusted in the ruler of governance that we represented, and it was an honour to serve.

We were warriors of light, peace and justice.

We fought with pride and honour.

We trusted in our brothers to fight and be strong.

We were more than friends; we were bonded as brothers to protect and honour one another, to keep each other safe from harm.

Battle after battle,

We walked and fought.

Rain, hail and shine,

strong to the divine,

we were united as one.

On further research, I found that around 7,000 soldiers were stationed on the Antonine Wall, from countries as far away as modern Syria, Spain, and Algeria.

These soldiers were made up of a mixture of:

Legionaries – These had to be Roman citizens over the age of 17. They would also need to be fighting fit as if you were too weak or too short, you would be rejected. As a legionary, you would be highly trained to be the best in infantry soldiers. Their duties would be to conquer and defend the Roman territories. They would have been armed with short swords, daggers, and javelins. They would have had helmets, shields and armour for protection.

Career soldiers – These would have achieved exceptional acts of bravery, enabling them to be promoted to a higher rank in the legion, such as commander, otherwise known as Legatus legionis. Each legion had their own commander and there were three known legions stationed in Britain during the Antonine period.

Auxiliary troops – These were the majority of the soldiers stationed at the wall. They were also known as the Roman army's cavalry. These men would not have been Roman citizens, although they would have been granted Roman citizenship once they retired.

These men would have been drawn into the Roman military system from across the empire, sometimes voluntarily, but often by force. They may have previously been farmers, labourers, or servants, just to name a few. They would attend weapons training every morning and would practice hand-to-hand combat with wooden swords, bows, slings and spears.

During their time at the wall, these men would have trained for battle, patrolled the wall, worshipped their god, helped to train others, and in some events, died. There would have also been some personal time for relaxation in their tents. Civilians would have been living alongside the soldiers at the wall, such as wives and children, as well as slaves, possibly of the commanding officers.

Rather than stone, the Antonine Wall consisted of a turf rampart 3-4 m high on a stone base, possibly topped with a timber palisade, fronted by a wide and deep ditch. The route of the wall made the most of the landscape, with ridges, hills, and slopes to create a forbidding barrier, much of which is still visible today. Forts along the wall provided accommodation for the troops and acted as secure crossing points.

All forts were linked by a road called the Military Way, which ran behind the rampart. (A rampart is a broad earthen mound surrounding a fortified place to protect it from artillery fire and infantry assault.)

When it was completed, the Antonine Wall was the most complex frontier ever built by the Roman army. It was the Romans' last linear frontier and was only occupied for about 20 years before it was abandoned in the AD 160s.

I am not a historian and I do not claim to be. I have written the channelled words from Spirit and spent time researching the information I have been given from my spirit guide, who I genuinely believe walked the Earth as a soldier or warrior during Roman times from his description.

Further reading for more information on The Antonine Wall can all be found at www.antoninewall.org.

These writings have given me hope and a real faith and trust in the divine spirit. I have asked these questions many times and read over the answers again and again. And it is with full trust in Spirit and in my heart that I now share these with you. I want to take you on this journey of knowing that we can connect with our spirit guide through writing and believing. We can build a true relationship with our spiritual guides and mentors to find out who they truly are and what our path is meant to be.

Is there anything else that you want to add here, Emanuel?

Lead the way on this journey of hope now, child.

Bring joy, love and happiness to others.

Be who you are here to be.

Embrace this lifetime on the earth.

Live life.

Walk in God's path.

We are here.

Many of us are here to guide you, and support you on this journey now.

What do you mean when you say 'walk in God's path'?

Do what is in your nature, for those who judge you do not know you.

Be good and kind.

Be humble and giving.

Give to others that they cannot do for themselves.

Share your light of love.

Amen Emanuel x

As I mentioned earlier, all the writings from Spirit are signed in this way. I'm not sure if Emanuel is my spirit guide's actual name or if this signature is used as a term of endearment, like ending a letter, 'With love from'... this is one question I have yet to ask. The Hebrew Bible shows that the word 'Amen' signifies certainty and truth, and Emanuel means, 'God is with us.'

We were connected before your birth into this lifetime, child.

We have been on many journeys together; I am your trusted friend.

We have lived and fought battles together.

We will again re-unite in time.

It has been a long journey to get you to this point, but I am glad that you are here.

Chapter Two

Why are you here now?

The world is entering a great time of transition and spiritual growth now, child. It is my will to call upon and touch the hearts of the Earth Angels and the white light workers who are already here on the earth, to now work in the wisdom of the light.

It a time for reconnection to the divine, an uprising of spiritual growth. There will be many important vibrational alignments or adjustments that will be happening here on the Earth now, child, as this is a new time for ascension. Our collective energies will be working together to reach new spiritual heights.

We have sent a calling all around the world, as this is a time for spiritual awakening, and we need helpers or teachers here on the Earth. To help work and share in the light of God. Many will have felt this calling within.

It was during the first coronavirus lockdown of 2020 that I felt my own calling, just as Emanuel mentions. Even though I had connected with him many times before, I knew this was different.

I had been invited by my good friend Gail to join her in a daily meditation practice. Through this practice, we would be following a program called the *21-Day Abundance Meditation Challenge*, by Deepak Chopra.

The focus of the programme was abundance, which, of course, is not all about money. Its aim was to help you to welcome an abundance of health, wealth, love, and prosperity into your life. It sounded like fun, and as I do love meditation, I didn't hesitate in accepting the invite. It was also during lockdown, so it was great to have a focus for something to do.

The meditation group was online, all set up and ready to go for us to begin.

There was a clear program of daily tasks and meditations to follow – I couldn't wait to get started! Each of the detailed tasks was to be completed before listening to the corresponding meditation. Once you have worked your way through the program, you should be able to identify the areas in your life that might be holding you back.

It is very clever in its approach and really helps you to clear away any negative thoughts or blockages surrounding you, to allow the full flow of abundance back into your life. If you have not already tried it, then I would highly recommend it. I set myself the challenge of completing each of the tasks first thing in the morning. It seemed like such a positive way to start the day.

It was during one of these daily meditation sessions that I sat up, bolt upright on my bed, and said out loud, 'I need to write this book.' Not only did I say the words, but I felt them and knew it was something I had to do. I'm not exactly sure if it was the daily practice of listening quietly that allowed me to hear the calling or if it was the intention of clearing away any negativity surrounding me at the time. But either way, I heard my calling, loud and clear.

Emanuel, you mentioned that you have sent a calling all around the world, and that you need helpers or teachers here on the Earth. Are you asking me to help you?

Why do you sound so surprised now, child? For you have chosen this journey in life, it's your chosen path for your inner Soul.

Together, we will share the words of wisdom for those who need guidance.

You will help to encourage others to have a clearer connection to the divine,

bringing forward the words from Spirit to heal their hearts and minds.

It's time to reignite the powerful healing light of love within our hearts.

It's a time to heal the Earth.

Can you explain this time of healing in a bit more detail, please?

The energies on the Earth are aligning now, child, for we are bringing balance and harmony with this change in vibration.

Your mankind is experiencing a time for great healing and letting go as you move towards the light. These vibrational changes are happening not only around you but also deep within you; it's part of your soul plan, the soul plan of many. We are opening your hearts and minds at this time to a new spiritual consciousness or spiritual growth within.

So, it is your intention for us to feel this change?

Yes, all around the world there will be significant and long-lasting changes ahead. These changes are for the greatest good now, child, for it is also a great time of inner questioning and finding peace within, as humanity strives

to remember who you are, and who you should be, or even stronger in a sense of who you are to become.

So, basically, you have sent us all a light bulb moment?

Ha ha! In a way, yes. We are shining our light like a torch to help inspire others to do the same.

There are many changes needed on the Earth, child, especially for Mother Earth herself. Gaia is calling for love, balance, and harmony to be restored and shown not only to the Earth, but for the environment that you live in, child, and for wellness in the air that you breathe.

It makes me sad to hear that Gaia is having to call out in this way. Can you guide us in what we need to do?

Show the Earth some newfound respect.

Be gentle with her, stop drowning her with all that you pour into the Earth.

Maybe humanity could think of her as a very old soul and look after her with consideration, as you would with one of your own elders.

Plant new seeds with love and kindness, that is all she asks.

Why have you called me now?

Just as we have called to many others now, child, as you know, we are connected in many ways.

In this time of change, I need a pure light essence to work through, to get my message across.

This is why I have been assigned to you, child.

Your lack of confidence in the beginning has now grown into full bloom. You have shown me that you have full trust, faith and belief in my words. This gives me hope.

The words that I ask you to share are for the good of all humanity.

May we have many years of working in spiritual truth together, sharing words of love and guidance to others.

Trust in this shift to a new world. My aim is the spread the love of God and the divine, shared into the hearts of many, all around the world. Blessed be.

You have heard your calling now, child, and I am here to assist you on your chosen path. Together, we can help inspire and create a new consciousness for Spirit to work through.

Although I feel very privileged to be asked to take on this role, I was, of course, having constant pangs of self-doubt and a fear of what this would mean for me.

Firstly, I am not a writer, and I have never really tried to write anything before, or not anything for public view, at least.

Secondly, I am being asked or called upon not to write just any old book, but to write a book through channelling words from Spirit.

And thirdly, I am being guided to share these words of wisdom with others. This is something that puts the fear of God into me!! Standing up to be seen and sharing the light.

I'm sure at this point you can share in my sense of fear in not only the responsibility but also the importance of sharing the message correctly. So, I gathered the many little journals that I have written with Emanuel over the years and read back over his words to reaffirm to myself that this is actually real. When I opened the first page, I was directed to this writing:

Emanuel, you have spoken many times about our chosen life path, but how do we know what that is?

Your many questions make me smile, child, as I don't think I have been asked as many with such interest for quite some time now; you bring joy to my heart.

As a soul or light being, child, you plan your journey to Earth long before you have even got here. Much planning and organisation is arranged before your soul enters a human body again to experience a lifetime on the Earth.

Your guides, ancestors, angels, and your higher self will have all gathered around you in council to help plan your journey; some may also have incarnated to the Earth with you, as to play a predominant role in your life story.

Your life plan is set up for you to experience spiritual growth and learning. Each plan is specific to each individual. And what you need to know. You will have many life lessons to learn and some karmic lessons, too, some of which you may not have completed from a previous lifetime and so brought forward again with you into this lifetime.

You will also have planned out specific dates and times along your chosen path. Once you reach each date or milestone, they will burst into light, like a firework in the sky, and transform into your planned experiences of both good and bad. These, in turn, will integrate with your chosen life learnings and open your awareness for spiritual growth.

When I was reading back over this information, I instantly felt like I was being pulled way back into a memory. It was like watching a video playing in front of my eyes: this was of a time around 2005 when I had been attending yet another event about angels. I mentioned earlier that I did spend a lot of time back then going to live talks and events whilst I was learning and gathering as much information as I could about spiritual things. This one was presented by a lady called Amy Biank, also now known as 'the intuitive angel'.

The talk was being held in a large conference room at one of our local hotels. I arrived a little late and so I quietly sneaked in at the back of the room. There were no seats left, so I stood in the back corner of the hall. All I could see in front of me was a sea of heads.

I remember being so surprised at the amount of people who had turned out – there must have been over 200 people in attendance. It really surprised me to learn that so many other people locally at the time were interested in angels too. I remember feeling quite overwhelmed as it was all very new and exciting.

Amy introduced herself and spoke all about angel connection. She captivated her audience as she spoke. As the evening progressed, Amy started to give messages directly to members of the audience. The messages were of guidance and comfort, and there were lots of tears and laughter all around the room. I was soaking up the atmosphere when I heard her say, 'I would like to come to you, the girl right at the back of the room.' I looked around thinking that she couldn't possibly mean me, but she said, 'Yes, you' as she pointed straight to me. 'I know that you can feel it in your heart,' she said, 'Yes, it's you I am coming to speak to.' I suddenly had the strangest feeling within me, a bit like having butterflies in your tummy. It was an inner knowing, a feeling like I had already met her, knew her, or had spoken to her before.

Amy went on to say, 'You are going to write a book,' and 'I also see you, standing here as I am now, sharing your words with others.'

She finished the message by saying, 'When you are called to work for the angels, you will feel this calling like no other.' I don't know why that memory had always stayed with me, but in that moment reading back over Emanuel's writings, it came straight back into the forefront of my mind.

I knew that he was showing me validation. With my newfound trust, I continued to ask ...

Emanuel, are you saying that we have pre-planned our everyday experiences, for example, of meeting people, going places, things that go wrong in our everyday lives?

Indeed, child.

When I attended that talk with Amy Biank or the one with Trudy Griswold, were they all pre-planned then?

Yes, I see that you are starting to understand the importance in this, the pre-planned synchronicities in life.

You may also have brought some life skills with you, too, that you have attained through previous lifetimes, child.

For your understanding, your life journey is like a map of the world: it is all set out, pre-planned and coded for reference, just as you would roll out a map and mark out the co-ordinates for your required destination. The difference here, child, is that your so-called co-ordinates are connected to your soul.

Your name you are each born to the earth with is also no coincidence, child.

Your name has already been chosen, as this is another part of your lifelong journey. You will find that each letter of your name reaches a specific vibration, a bit like hitting a high chord in music notes. These vibrations when reached are a true reflection of your souls' true intention for this lifetime. The date, time and place you are born to the Earth is also known as your destiny.

Your soul path journey, you see, is already written.

Emanuel, I love this information; is there anything else you can share about this, please?

I love your enthusiasm; I feel the lift in your vibration as your soul sings, as you know this to be true.

As human beings, you still of course have the choice of free will. In most cases, you will deviate from your path from time to time and we will gently nudge you back. There are some, of course, that will never fulfil their chosen path here on the Earth and, as such, will return to God to choose another life plan and experience the cycle of life once again. You each, in turn, will continue to have further lives on the Earth, until you have fulfilled all your life's chosen lessons, or karma as it is also known. When all has been completed, we call this ascension, and you need not walk the Earth again. You would become a spiritual teacher or guide as you know them.

Your pre-planned journey is not meant to be effortless or problem-free, and at times it may also bring you feelings of great hurt or disappointment. With this in mind, please remember, child, that your vibrational numbers are created for you to bring a vast amount of life experiences, some of which are love, kindness, compassion, relationships, betrayal and trust. It is in the most challenging of these experiences that will help you to grow into the human being that you have incarnated here to be.

Your soul path is calling you, child, so I encourage you now to stand up to be the person you are here to be.

I now fully understand why Emanuel is here, at this time. It is not just a part of my soul plan, but it is also a part of yours. Your destiny is intwined with mine, and as you are now reading this book, you will have felt your own calling, too.

Through Emanuel's words, we will be sharing in his spiritual wisdom, which will help you to receive the words of clarity and love from Spirit that will guide you onto the rest of your own soul path journey.

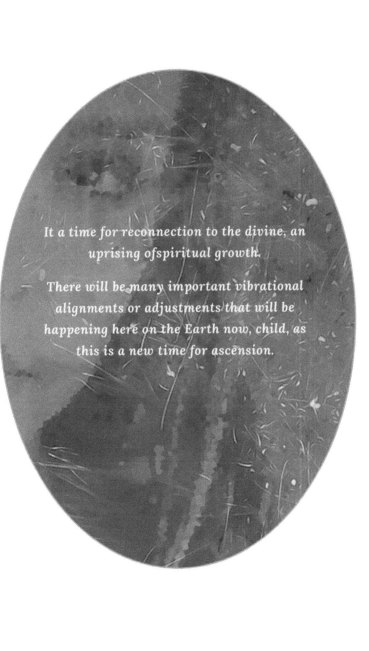

It a time for reconnection to the divine, an
uprising ofspiritual growth.

There will be many important vibrational
alignments or adjustments that will be
happening here on the Earth now, child, as
this is a new time for ascension.

CHAPTER THREE

WHAT DO YOU WANT TO SAY IN YOUR BOOK, EMANUEL?

I thank you, my child, for the opportunity to share my wisdom of inner light and knowledge.

I am here to share in my love of humanity and share through this message the light of love for all.

My aim is to shine the essence of beauty through all the words to be written here, so we may touch the hearts and souls of those who are reading. Blessed be.

I bring forward the words for hope, which are to be shared around the world with great purpose.

Firstly, I bring you blessings from the many souls that have returned home. And I share with you their eternal love and wisdom to be delivered straight to the hearts of their loved ones still here on the Earth.

I ask you to open your heart to accept the love and joy that surrounds you in the now.

I ask you to affirm in your beliefs of the life hereafter.

I am guiding you to trust, believe and have faith in the light of God, always.

I aim to help you understand the new expansion of existence in this ever-changing time.

What is the new expansion of existence that you mention?

The love and the spiritual connection that is growing between worlds now, child.

The connection between souls is expanding; we are calling for this to happen now.

We are creating, you are creating.

We are being aligned together now to create together the new and harmonious world ahead.

Thus, in its existence, it should be full of spiritual connections and spiritual beliefs, holding onto a strong faith in the divine.

We are inviting you to feel the new opportunities that await by letting go of the old, to allow the new.

There is an essence in the air you are all breathing, creating a new you and a new belonging in the universe.

We are growing into a new and spiritual dimension.

I feel positive about the future of humanity on the Earth.

Kindness and humility are being restored.

You are a changing world right now and it is for the good of all.

White light is shining through the hearts of many.

Be the change.

Welcome the bridge to this dimension, for many souls are to travel.

What do you mean by 'welcome the bridge'?

The doorway to connect with Spirit, the bridge allows us to connect and pass through.

Whether new souls are arriving or old souls are returning, it is called home.

The doorways to our dimensions are aligning now.

You are getting ready for a new light of consciousness.

What is this new light of consciousness, please?

A new time of sensing the soul.

You are merging with Spirit and the flow of all life,

a oneness with the universe.

What would you say is a strong faith in the divine, Emanuel?

God, child, God.

Whomever or whatever you choose to call it.

It's funny – I never really thought of myself as a believer in God. My first introduction, as I remember, was as a child when my grandmother used to take me along to her local church for the Sunday school service. It was here that I was introduced to the usual children's Bible stories such as David and Goliath, John the Baptist, the birth of Christ, Adam and Eve – you know the script. I remember huddling round in a group for the story time, listening to all the tales which are full of purpose.

In reflection, as a child you really have no idea of the full extent of the word 'god', or the true importance in any of the Bible stories that we are told, whether that be at church or through school.

I have often wondered if these are just stories that have been embellished through the years with bit and bits added on like a game of Chinese whispers. All the same, I do believe these first Bible stories or nativity plays are a good learning experience, an introduction to something more, something ethereal, which will lead us into some of the questions we have or tend to develop as an adult in relation to our own beliefs in Spirit.

My grandmother even bought me my very own hymn book way back in 1987, signed with love from her, something I have kept safe and close to my heart. In honesty, though, I have had a wee giggle here and there about that: I must have enjoyed the hymns rather that the service, as it wasn't a Bible she bought me, just a hymn book!!

From memory, my favourites are the hymns which mention the angels, like 'Hark the Herald Angels Sing'. Whenever I hear this song, I feel that it really does reach out to uplift and empower the soul.

When I was a teenager at school, we had the usual end-of-term church services to attend, but that was about the extent of my church-going. My knowledge of religion, pretty basic. I wasn't really that interested back then, and throughout our church service, there was no real elaboration on the angels or the realms of Spirit from the minister, as far as I can remember. So, nothing to hold my attention.

It's funny how, years later, you are drawn back to spirituality. Without question, as when Emanuel mentions God, it just seems right or accepted that it is just so.

I don't think any of us realise that for the main part of our lives, we are already a part of divine plan or journey with Spirit. Most people think that God is upstairs somewhere, or around us somehow, but have been taught to know that he or the angels will be there when we need them most.

When you are called onto your path of spirituality, it's a bit like an opening of a door. A new door to endless opportunity. You start to experience a rapid growth of interest in spiritual things, and you might start going to church for the first time in your life. You start reading spiritually-themed books. You are starting to seek for answers to reconnect to the divine for your own spiritual growth.

How would you describe God from a spiritual sense, Emanuel?

All God is one God.

We all believe in an essence of light.

God is the creator of all things.

No matter who you believe your god is, the pure energy of love will always touch your heart

God does not create war.

Men who desire power and greed use the word of God to fuel their desires for power and strength.

This fighting for purpose begins –

Who is the most powerful, most feared?

This desire to fight with the essence of God is a path chosen, a path to walk, that will lead to only pain and suffering for all those around. Many blessings are sent to help in these situations.

God's essence will always try to restore the balance of peace.

The energy of God surrounds you and is within you; connect with this light for everlasting love, light, and happiness within.

Your use of the words, 'this fighting for purpose begins' stands out strongly to me here,

Do you think this was why we were fighting when we were soldiers together?

Yes, child; power, expansion and growth.

We believed it was God's will or the will of the gods.

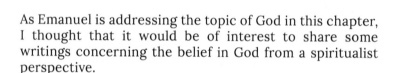

As Emanuel is addressing the topic of God in this chapter, I thought that it would be of interest to share some writings concerning the belief in God from a spiritualist perspective.

By spiritualist, I mean that we share in the belief that communication with a spiritual dimension outside our Earth plane is possible. A dimension which is a host to our angels, spirit guides and ancestors. Being spiritual offers us a willingness to be open and surrounds us with the endless possibilities of the greater good, rather than setting out a specific set of religious beliefs.

We also share the belief that when we leave this Earth, we return to Spirit consciousness, this spiritual dimension allows communication between this world and the etheric realms.

Please feel free to substitute another word for 'God' here –whatever resonates with you, whether that be Spirit, angels, being of light, etc. We are not relating to Christianity here, Buddhism, Sikhism, Hinduism, Islam, or any specific religion. We are relating to God as a higher consciousness that presides over all of us. All religions are essentially manmade. We are not born into this lifetime here on the earth with a religion or faith, but our inner soul leads us to find our own path of belief and enlightenment along the way.

As believers in the divine, we often refer to God as the

divine Spirit, the great Spirit, the cosmos, beings of light, or even 'the man upstairs'.

God is often described as the eternal source of all life, a divine creative energy.

God is the natural flow of the universe which expands, sustains and nurtures all creation.

Spiritual beings do not have a physical body as we do, but nevertheless, we all Spirit.

These words here made me understand in simple terms that, for example, 'As the earth is changing from season to season, it is clear to see that the energy of Spirit is within everything. The sun shining, the grass growing the flowers blooming. The absolute beauty in everything that surrounds us is from the creator or the divine Spirit.'

I feel as if I should burst into song with the hymn, 'All Things Bright and Beautiful' on that note! I really want to highlight to you today that even though we can sometimes feel overwhelmed at the possibilities of our spiritual path, God is always with us.

God is around us, as God is love and light. An energy that flows within the natural flow of the universe. It manifests in all things. This creative life force energy we call God or the divine Spirit has created LIFE, in all its forms: bugs, bees, trees, the fish in the sea. You and me and, of course, the universe itself. This universal life force keeps our existence in a state of balance, allowing expansion, transformation, and creation to take place. Isn't that amazing?

We are creators. Just as God has created the universe and all of life.

God is not only in the beauty that surrounds us; he is within us, and you are free to celebrate this energy in your own way.

Which leads me to my next question for Em.

Do you need to believe in God to live a spiritual life, Emanuel?

Ahh my child, this is a very good question; my heart sings with glee, I am overjoyed as you are really starting to think this through and welcome the endless possibilities we share with Spirit.

No, you do not have to believe in God to live or have an interest in a spiritual life.

What do YOU think that being spiritual is, child?

I think being spiritual means you are good and kind and would do no harm to others.

My elaboration on that child, would be spiritual means from the heart,

a heart felt feeling that offers

Love

Kindness

Compassion

Joy

Sharing

Giving.

To be able to give and receive unconditional love truly from the heart, is what I believe to be a spiritual essence or being in your life form.

Have an open heart and mind to allow to the possibilities that there is something greater in which we are a part of. This openness will draw the light of the divine to you; it will lead you on your path.

I noticed that you mentioned feeling from the heart previously – can you explain a bit more of what you mean by this, please?

Your heartfelt centre is very powerful, child, for this is the bridge between your earthly and spiritual aspirations. The heart is where we connect with love within, and the universal love of the divine.

Put your hand on your heart now and feel the power in each beat. Your heart within powers your body to give it life. It also powers your emotions of love, compassion, and kindness for yourself and for others. By connecting your mind and inner spirit through energy, you can create from the heart centre.

This is where you will find your connection with Spirit at its stronges;t also, it is the centre of your awareness. When the heart is open, you will feel deeply connected to Spirit.

So, basically, you are telling us to open our hearts to heal. Let go of any old hurts, emotions, or heartbreaks which surround our hearts, or emotions such as grief that we are holding onto, in order to have a better connection to Spirit.

Yes, child, in a way I am. Always open your heart to receive the endless possibilities of Spirit.

Open your heart to align and create with the universal energy of love.

Open your heart to God.

Inner Light Meditation to Open Your Heart

Sit in an upright position

With your feet firmly planted on the floor

Take a few deep breaths as you begin

Imagine the connection to your soul

And deep within your centre is the essence of energy

A spark of light

As you welcome the light of God around you

Move your consciousness away from your mind

To the centre of your being

You are connecting to the essence of divinity within you

And as you open your heart to receive

Allow your inner light to reignite

Accept it to be so

Allow the essence of who you truly are to emanate
through your body

As it expands

Down into your arms and upper body

Flowing and expanding into your hips and flowing
through your legs and feet

as it sweeps through you and expands beyond you

Feel the energy through every part of your being

As you move the energy out to your aura, feel how this energy expands

As you touch the sun, the moon and the stars

Feel completely filled with the light of who you are

This is the power of you

As you feel the energy vibration

Feel on the outside of the aura

the energy of the divine light of God

Connecting with you now

As you breathe in this energy that surrounds you, you are becoming one with the divine

Allow this energy to nourish you

As you surrender to the light and let go of the old

Your heart is open, your heart is free, your heart is full of love

You are safe

You are loved

You are so

Take a few deep breaths now and bring yourself gently back

As you return to centre

Take a few moments to wiggle your fingers and toes

As you return fully awake and re-energised from the session

You said earlier that you feel positive about humanity on the earth now; what do you mean by that?

Humankind is one of a kind.

You are unique,

each and every one of you.

You have a learning to do.

The more you learn, the faster you ascend.

Although you can deviate from your chosen life path,

eventually, you will find your way back.

Many souls choose their experiences.

Pain

Illness

Strength

Courage

Determination

Compassion.

What about cruelty?

We do not condone cruelty to others. If you are cruel or harm others with intention, then the karmic laws shall bring these deeds back into balance. Those true to the light in their soul will bring a journey of light to their life.

Why do we need to feel different emotions?

The emotions you feel at times of sadness, hurt, upset, tears of crying and despair, are all within our deepest moments. It is here when we are learning and growing the most. Expanding our human experiences.

All lessons and experiences here on Earth are for your ascension.

Why is humanity changing in this time, as you say?

Throughout all of humanity, you are growing at a rapid pace at the moment,

with an opening of your hearts and minds, you are willing to change.

You are realigning with your soul's journey

in a new expansion of time that you are ready to receive.

Many of you are awakening to feel this call.

How do you know if you feel it?

Some of you may be walking on your own path totally oblivious to the soul growth and in this time without ever feeling the recognition of this call.

You may be walking your individual journey as part of a heartfelt or heart-led journey alone, rather than your spiritual one at this time.

Some humans on the Earth in this lifetime may never believe, connect, or speak to their own guides. This is also ok, as this is a part of their own encounter. There is nothing wrong in experiencing their own humanity in this way.

In short, this is just a slower path for their ascension. I would expect that many lifetimes may be repeated here, over and over again until the inner recognition of the true soul or the inner being is reignited.

As your Spiritual guides and mentors,

we are here, as your trusted friends.

We are here, to touch the hearts of humanity,

To bring joy and healing into your hearts.

We are here to help encourage and enlighten you

by sharing in this opportunity to expand your belief system with faith.

We are encouraging all of humanity to connect with their own beautiful spirit mentors,

through writing, journaling, or meditation practice.

We will help you to connect with the higher self to bring inner peace, comfort and joy into your life once again.

I welcome this opportunity to teach as this makes my heart sings with joy.

You are getting ready for a new light of
consciousness.

A new time of sensing the soul.

You are merging with Spirit and the flow of
all life, a oneness with the universe.

CHAPTER FOUR

HUMANITY AND CLARITY

Emanuel, as we have been talking about humanity, can you share a little more about you and your life here on Earth, please?

This is kind of you to ask now, child – of course.

I have lived on the Earth throughout many different lifetimes.

I have reincarnated again and again, always being reborn into a similar lifetime.

I now understand that it was my soul journey or a requirement for my own soul growth.

I was repeating my journey of life, the circle of life to fight and fight again until I accepted God into my heart, or until I surrendered to God.

And this is so, on the journey of our own connection here, that I speak of in this book.

We lived and worked in a town just outside Pirus; it was a few miles from the market town of Centri.

I was the son of a farmer.

We worked hard for the land.

I was a tall and strong boy.

My father joked with me about the muscles I grew on my arms.

My father was named Otto and my mother Maria.

I had an older brother Cassius and a sister called Mariel.

This path you ask me to walk, back into my lifetime, into this memory is good for me, child, as it has been such a long time ago; it is warming to rekindle with my once earthly presence.

We had a humble lifestyle with little to eat or drink.

We worked hard and sold what we could from our land to stay strong.

We had animals too. I recall a bull to pull the cart with hay to the barn.

We had barley and oats – mmm, I can still smell here with this memory.

The hay made my eyes stream, but the oats filled my belly.

There was much love and laughter which surrounded us; we were bonded by love.

I was still just a boy when my father died.

My older brother took charge and looked after the farm for my mother and my sister.

It was a hard life.

Our hard work, our food supply, was often stolen from us by strangers; they would come from the sea, and we could not understand why this would happen time and time again.

We would pray, but God did not help us.

I was angry with life, and I started to fight for vengeance. I had a strong anger within me,

grief from the loss of my father, as I understand it now. But I did not know what this inner burning was then.

I longed for pain as my bodily pain would relinquish the pain felt in my heart.

This is what led me to try to become a soldier.

The pride and honour in grace a gift from the gods, I thought.

My mother and my sister were heartbroken, but my brother shook my hand with pride

as I left on my journey.

I never returned home to see my family again once my plight began.

I cried tears of joy and of sadness as I left, as I especially loved my sister Mariel dearly.

She was a beautiful soul, full of joy,

but my journey of faith was to begin.

My, I feel weary as I think of this journey as it was long and lonely at times, but it brought justice into my heart.

Thank you for sharing this, Em. It's wonderful to know some details of your life. May I ask, what was your earthly name at this time, can you remember?

Yes, I remember, child; my name was Martikus. They called me Martikus the Fortem.

(I took a little time to research the word fortem, and I discovered it means 'brave' in Latin, which made me smile.)

Did you have a wife, or did you get married at all?

No, my child, for this was forbidden as a soldier; you were married to God or the gods as we knew them, and to the empire that we served. I did have a love though, or should I say, I shared in the love of a woman. Her name was Grace. My heart sings with glee as I remember her; she had light coloured hair and the softest skin. I loved her, child, I loved her.

Why could you not marry her?

As I said, it was forbidden at this time, child. But you do not need marriage to share in love, the exchange of two hearts, the connection of two souls, as this is bound by time alone.

Can you describe the feeling of love to me?

Ha ha, child, for you do make me laugh at times; love is not a description. It is a feeling within, a feeling like no other. This feeling is only true to you, connected to your soul and that of your soulmates.

Eternal love runs through every essence of your being; it's a timeless connection between you.

Why do you think the feeling of love is so important to us?

This is one of the most important experiences that you can feel in your lifetime,

to love and feel loved.

It gives you a sense of belonging.

It connects the heart, mind and soul.

It is unconditional and free to all.

True love is eternal and will pass the dimensions of time.

Did you ever have any children?

No, child, there were no children here in this lifetime.

That seems sad to me. Did you ever get annoyed that you could not live your life as you wanted?

This is a good question child, but remember it was not love that I was looking for, child – it was vengeance, as my heart was full of anger, child, and the fight or fighting was my one and only love or passion.

When we are working together on this book, I feel that Emanuel is taking me on my own journey of faith as we write each word; it an ongoing building of trust in one another through our conversations.

I started to research for a Roman town called Pirus, but there was nothing. I was so disappointed as I was sure that this was correct. I looked and looked again. I was just about to give up on it when Em suggested, *change the spelling*. So, I continued to alter the spelling until eventually I realised that by adding the extra vowels of A and E it would lead me to Piraeus.

Piraeus does indeed have a long history pertaining to ancient Greece. It was a port town which connected to the centre – or as Emanuel said, *Centri* – of Athens. Piraeus has been inhabited since at least the 26th century BC. Athens is one of the oldest named cities in the world, and became the leading city of ancient Greece in the first millennium BC.

With all this compelling information coming to me, I was also receiving a recurring thought. It was persistent, just like hearing a record repeating itself. It was telling me that I should source out a medium who could offer spiritual drawings, or to be more specific, a drawing of my spirit guide. I decided to honour the nudge from Spirit, and even though I thought it was going to be a bit of a gamble to find someone with such a skill, I started the search all the same.

I started out by looking on the internet, as we do. I typed 'spirit guide artists' into the Google search bar, crossed my fingers and hoped for the best. Lo and behold, a few people popped up on the screen. In my sheer delight, I followed the leads onto social media. As I was looking for inspiration, I really wanted something or someone to jump out at me and catch my attention, to let me know this was the correct business or person for the task in hand.

My search continued over the next few weeks, and I had managed to narrow down the list to just a few. I thoroughly researched their businesses or social media pages for information on their spiritual talents, and I really took the time to read up on their previous client reviews, but still, no one. Or nothing that certainly caught my attention in the way of the light bulb moment I was looking for.

I had almost given up on the idea when I discovered The Wellness Foundry on Instagram by an absolute fluke. I was searching for wellness ideas – as we were in the middle of a pandemic, any ideas for stress relief or meditation techniques were a must-have. Then, boom! On Instagram, here was a medium who offered tarot readings and spirit guide drawings. I was so excited to investigate further. I found the business profile so inviting, and I instantly felt very drawn to Finogal Greenwell. There was such a gentleness in his profile images that reached out to me, inviting me to make contact with him. I knew there and then that this was it – he was the person that I had been looking for to do my spirit guide drawing. I started following his page, just to see what it was all about. Everything on the page looked professional and well presented. So, as I trusted this nudge from Spirit, I went on to book a spirit guide drawing session with him.

The reading appointment was arranged as a Zoom call session on a Saturday afternoon. I only had to enter the details of my name to confirm the booking, and no other questions were asked prior to the session.

When I connected with Finogal for the session, I was instantly relaxed by his warming charm and welcome expression. He was dressed in a white shirt and surrounded by ethereal light.

Finogal clearly explained to me the how the session would be set up, and in which way he would be working. He explained that he would firstly connect with a loved one for me, and then continue on with one of my spirit guides. I have to say, I was about to burst with excitement as the session commenced. I knew how important this session was not only for me but also for Emanuel, and the validation in being seen.

Just before the session started, I do confess to saying a little prayer out very loud, asking for Emanuel to please step froward for the session to be seen, as it was so important for me to have this validation.

As Finogal began the session, he instantly connected with my grandmother. He gave me a clear description of her appearance and went onto describe her personality. I was in no doubt that it was her. As he was passing on the message from her, he was also sketching her picture. I was enthralled by the clarity of words he was sharing with me; it was all very accurate for what was going on in and around my life at the time.

We were off to a great start, and as he moved into the spirit guide session, my heart raced with anticipation as I could not wait to hear what he was going to say.

Just as Finogal was just about to move on from my grandmother and onto the spirit guide connection, I clearly saw with my own mind's eye or inner vision Emanuel stepping in behind him, just where he was sitting. As I watched Em step forward to blend with Finogal,

Finogal actually looked over his shoulder at exactly the same time, as he obviously felt the energy from Emanuel moving forward to connect with him, too. This made me gasp a little, seeing this in motion on the screen with my own eyes. It gave me goosebumps.

Here is the discussion between myself and Finogal from the spirit guide session. I have presented this as a script for easy reading so you can see that I hardly said a word as I didn't want to give the game away.

Fiongal: Your spirit guide is a man.

Me: Okay.

Finogal: I feel that he is a knight or soldier.

Me: Oh, really?

Finogal: Yes, but not a 'knight in shining armour' kind of knight. He was a warrior. He fought battles and liked to fight, yes, he enjoyed the thrill of the fight, especially the 'Charge'. He is telling me here that he lived many lifetimes, always as a soldier. He died again and again and in more than one battle.

Me: This is very interesting.

Fionogal: He has been a soldier in lots of different forms; he is showing me a tapestry from 1066.

As a Norman or Normandy, I think this is connected to the battle of Hastings.

Oh, I think he has also been a Viking, and a Roman. There are so many aspects of this guide being shown to me; it's like he has lived life after life, battle after battle, and all have been lived as a different form of similar character, as a barbarian or warrior-type character. It is like he is showing me his blueprint of himself. Like the layering of one on top of another, as I see him changing from life to life and he was always living as a man.

Me: This is amazing information, thank you.

(I was actually thinking, 'Oh my god!! He has actually made the connection with Emanuel here!')

Fionogal: As he shows me here, this aspect of him, he is a bigger, muscular, barbarian, carnal man, full of rage and aggression. Oh, in one lifetime here, he is showing me that he died with an arrow through his eye.

Me: Oh, my goodness.

Fiongal: He says, he had to learn soul maturity for growth. For these aspects of him, the warrior in him, now no longer exist as they have not integrated into who he is now.

He says, 'I didn't care whose side I was on – I just wanted to fight. I have no embarrassment about it and will not apologise in sharing, for this is a true aspect of what I was and who I was.

Oh, he is very straight to the point, and I like that.

Me: Do you know what type of guide he is?

Finogal: He is not a gatekeeper; he is a guide who is helping you.

He gives you strength and the ability to push through and the power to stand in the face of knowing, trusting your intuition or sense of knowing.

I feel he is not a moral guide and is not here to judge you. Instead, he brings strength and determination; he wants you to stand up to be seen. He brings encouragement to get the job done.

As I am drawing him, I see his helmet and the nose guard.

He is associated with the colour red and some sort of gold or yellow colour on there, too.

He is a fire-based connection, so to honour him, light a candle.

Call upon him for strength, an energy burst or vigour.

He helps to remove barriers or blockages.

He likes to get stuff out of the way with great vigour.

He is encouraging us to connect with the divine masculine.

He is like the emperor card from the tarot deck.

He says that sometimes we need aggression and strength in our lives, and if this is harnessed correctly, it can help us to push through the most difficult of life experiences.

Spirit drawing is not something that I practice regularly, but way back around the time when I started to read *Angel Speak*, when I also had my very first writing with Emanuel as I detail in Chapter One, I made three separate drawings.

One was for a close friend at the time. We were both really into Reiki, crystals and angels. We had been on a mini workshop for spirit drawings, and she asked if I could try to do a drawing for her. This was something I had never attempted before but agreed to give it a go. The picture turned out to be of an American Indian guide with a clear feather braided in his hair.

The second drawing was for another friend. She had recently separated from her husband, and I was trying to tune in and draw a picture of a new partner she was yet to meet. I drew a picture of a dark-haired gentleman whom neither of us recognised at the time. However, a few months later, the picture turned out to be of my very own soul mate, who is now my husband.

The third drawing was of my own spirit guide. I had not known this was Emanuel at the time. But I drew a picture of a bold soldier, wearing a helmet with distinctive a nose guard.

Funnily enough, from then onwards, I never tried to draw with Spirit again.

Back to Finogal, who had finished his drawing and turned the page to the screen to reveal the picture. I was absolutely gobsmacked by the accuracy. Here in front of me was basically the same drawing that I had sketched of Emanuel myself at least 16 years prior to this sitting. He was wearing the exact helmet with the nose guard as I had previously seen, the square jawline and rugged edges – it was him! I stared at this for a few moments, almost in disbelief. Between the portrait and the words he had spoken, Finogal's demonstration was so outstanding that I felt overcome with joy at the validation. This moment is certainly noted as one of my favourite confirmations from Spirit.

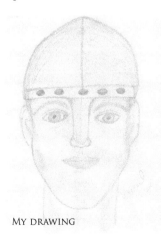

MY DRAWING

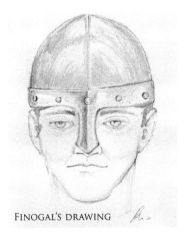

FINOGAL'S DRAWING

During the session, Finogal also described the uniform in detail, which was worn by The Legion Legio VI Victrix. These were one of the Roman legions stationed at Westerwood Fort and the legion I believe we were a part of. Their campaign was represented with a red background with a gold bull-shaped emblem in place to represent strength.

As we brought the session to a close, we exchanged our thanks to both of our spiritual helpers and sat for a moment to absorb the high vibe energy that remained.

In the days to follow, all I could think was:

Wow!!

16 years later!! Amazing that someone you have never met can connect with your own spirit guide in this way. So, for me, this was a total confirmation of the validity of spirit communication and how we can connect and work with them in so many different ways.

I feel fortunate to have made this timely connection with Finogal and truly blessed to be working with Emanuel, who has certainly showed great patience in his waiting for me to work with him.

This is one of the most important
experiences that you can feel in your
lifetime, to love and feel loved.

It gives you a sense of belonging.

It connects the heart, mind and soul.

It is unconditional and free to all.

True love is eternal and will pass the
dimensions of time.

CHAPTER FIVE

Let Go

Surrender

Be Free

Be Happy

As I share the details with you on how I lived many lifetimes, child,

I also want to share through this teaching the knowledge that I have gained from my ascension.

When you surrender all of your inner hurting, worry, anger, grief, stress or anxiety here, in all that surrounds you in this daily life, then you can be truly free to walk this path on Earth. In alignment for the journey that we are sent here to be on.

Are you saying here, Emanuel, that we need to experience both sides of life, the good and the bad, for progression?

Yes, child.

It is in your daily life's struggles that you are receiving, receiving from the universe.

I know that this does not feel just at times. I understand from my own life experience that it seems incomprehensible here, that all of the injustices and struggles that you face are lessons for you to experience and grow from.

When we do not listen or accept the journey,

when we do not have a willingness to learn or change,

when we are blaming others for our experiences,

when we are being a victim,

then we cannot move forward with our life plan.

(This paragraph really struck a chord with me, and I started to look at some of my own life experiences here, as I am sure you will be considering yours in this moment, too.)

We all have experienced many things in our own life's journey. Some are positive and some are negative or hurtful, whether this has been from our first broken heart, the ending of a relationship or a sudden bereavement. Maybe you have met the love of your life or have just been offered the opportunity of a lifetime. We hold our experiences within our hearts.

How do we move forward from our experiences, Em?

We must surrender.

We must let go.

We must open our hearts to receive.

Often our experiences will break us down, bit by bit, so that we have nowhere else to turn but to trust in Spirit.

Often you will find, those that have a connection or communication with Spirit will have had the most difficult of life experiences. In this case, often this connection to Spirit will come to them as a gift later into their lives, when they have reached an age to accept it as so.

Yes, as without this, you may never be willing to open your heart to receive or hear our calling. It can be those with the hardest of experiences to endure that have or will experience the strongest connection to Spirit.

****

I believe this to be true. I have had many experiences throughout my own life, good and bad. There have been times where I have thought, 'Is there anything else possible that the universe could throw at me?' I see here from Emanuel's words that sometimes we need to have these experiences to help us trust in Spirit, to strengthen our beliefs and help us to open our hearts to the love of the divine.

I would like to share this little journaling exercise with you. I found it helpful with letting go some of my own life experiences. I'm sure it will help you to open and heal your hearts, too.

You will need to have pen and paper – I like to have a journal dedicated to my spiritual work.

Take a moment to write down all your most important life experiences. Start with a list of ideas, such as:

Best Day Ever

Love and Romance

Saddest Moment

Worst Day Ever

and so on. Write each of these ideas at the top of its own page in our notebook, and then under each idea, write out your experience.

For example:

Best Day Ever – The happiest day of my life was when I got married.

Saddest Moment – The saddest day of my life was when my

father died.

In this moment, look within to consider your life events, and write them all down in detail.

Relive in this moment the happiest and most heart-warming of them. Draw in and hold these memories close. Now, focus on how your heart feels in this moment.

Hold onto this feeling within you as, and Emanuel says – Let's surrender.

Say:

I open my heart to receive the love from the universe.

I thank you for all the good and happy memories I hold close to me now.

As I take time to remember the joy,

I am ready, I am willing, I am open

to receive the new and positive opportunities that await me.

I am now ready to let go of any sad or negative experiences that have surrounded me in my life.

I allow my heart to heal, I allow myself to forgive, I allow myself to be free.

I have faith

I have joy

I allow my heart to heal

As I open my heart to receive

Eternal love from the universe

I surrender

I would like to talk about karma here, child, for it is not the will of God or the path of the soul to intentionally hurt or cause physical pain to others.

This is not welcomed lightly into the house of God.

Karma is an essence, not only for the bad, but it is also for the good.

The weak show their true weakness by intentionally hurting another.

You need strength and power to always offer kindness in your heart.

The karmic flow of the universe will retain the memory of the real-life journey that you chose to live on the Earth now, child.

You have, of course, free will and it is your own free will that can take you on the path of destruction – self-destruction or the destruction of others.

There is no ascension for this behaviour.

The soul will return again and again until the lessons from this have been re-done.

Karma comes from the Sanskrit word *karam*, meaning 'action'.

Karmic law, as Emanuel mentions here, talks of the consequences that are held upon our actions.

Another way of looking at it is our words and actions create cause and effect.

Other words that are used to describe karma are:

Fate

Destiny

Kismet

Luck

Fortune

Divine will.

Most of us already have preconceived ideas of karma, through popular phrases, such as:

What goes around comes around

You reap what you sow

You get what you give

and so on and so forth. The philosophy of karma is shared across multiple religions all around the world. The karmic journey is not just about being perfect all of the time; it is recognising what no longer serves us here in this life and using the good karma to undo what has been, to become who we really are through continued thought or actions.

So, why is it that even though we believe in karma, it always seems to let us down when we need it most?

This is a very good question, child. Why, indeed?

Karma is not good or bad; it is just working and aligning with the divine laws of the universe.

Allow me to explain further here, child.

As human on Earth, you have free will. You may choose how you react or respond to every life instance.

You are free to make your own life choices and you alone have the personal responsibility for those.

God does not stop mankind's creation of world wars or hatred or abuse from happening as we on Earth create our own wrongdoings. We are each accountable for our actions and we must take responsibility for them.

Karma is not always about the bad; is it also about the good.

Karma is one of the divine laws of the universe and is simply here to help us to restore balance.

Balancing the scales of life, it takes everything on our journey full circle, until it falls back into balance or where it is meant to be... back on the soul path.

Karma is not something to be scared of, as if you are always giving out good, then good will be returned to you.

It will always bring you what you deserve, good and bad, whilst keeping you on your soul path's journey. We are all a part of a bigger picture, and it keeps us aligned to that.

The universal laws of life.

Karma is not letting you down as you asked her, child; the outcome may be of a higher plan and just no part of your journey in this very moment.

I hope that makes sense.

Yes, it does, thank you.

What are the divine laws of the universe that you mention here, please?

This is an important part of your journey and the journey of wisdom to be shared. The universal laws are not to be broken, however once you understand them in full, which is my aim in these teachings, then you can introduce the elements from these into your daily life. You will allow the flow of change into your heart. They are the principles that preside over everyone and everything, the rules of the universe.

Ok, so how do we start to introduce them into our daily lives?

Understanding, it's all about understanding.

If it is all about understanding, then how would YOU describe the laws of the universe, Em? I have been looking into these, and I am confused, as some say there are 7, some say 12 and others say 10. Do you know why that is or why are there so many options?

As you know, child, each person will relay a story in a different way. We each have a different way of explaining things and so there is no right or wrong here; you will just draw or create the universal law which pertains to you at the correct time.

Such as the law of grace, this one I hold dear to my heart, child, for this is one of importance and meaning. For here you can create or be the creator within, but only when you are ready for recognising that your every word, every thought, or every deed leads to creation or manifestation. We can invoke this wonderful spiritual law of grace. Once you have recognised that we have created all of our situations or experiences through our consciousness, then you are ready to receive the law of grace.

We can offer grace to others by our words and actions such as compassion, mercy, empathy, forgiveness, and unconditional love. And when you have opened your heart to another, we can in turn receive this love. When we open our hearts with compassion, the love you emanate to another will also allow your own heart to heal. Forgiveness, of course, is another action of kindness which dissolves and transforms negativity. Forgiveness results in emotional and physical healing for the giver and the receiver. The law of grace allows this healing to occur as the high vibrational energies of love overturns the lower energies of pain and fear for further expansion of the soul's learning.

Your spirit guides or spiritual helpers especially work with grace when they are encouraging you to say or do that which will distract from any negative outcomes. Which brings us back again to your personal choice.

Are you saying here that we can only action the law of grace once we recognise that we are the creators of our own experiences?

Yes, essentially, child, I am. I am guiding you and teaching you to recognise your life's experiences and to learn from them to grow. So, you can create essentially the life that you are here to live.

Full of joy, full of hope and full of happiness.

As Spirit, this is all we want you to achieve:

growth, love, learning and experience.

What would you say are the other most important laws, or which are of the most benefit to us?

Each of the laws are of importance, to bring and restore balance at all times. Should I have to choose the best for humanity, I would say The Law of Free Will, my child. You have the power to choose, you have the power to make a decision, right or wrong. And the final outcome is yours and yours alone. Spirit may help to inspire you through vivid dreams or gentle whispers into your ears or mind, but the final decision on which choice or path you choose is essentially your own.

We are all spiritual beings here, child. You are just having a bodily experience, a bodily experience on the Earth, but you are still connected always to the divine source. When you arrived on the Earth, you may have forgotten this aspect of yourself. In this time, we are awakening all the souls are reminding them of who they are – thus, this great surge in collective energy that surrounds us now. This raise in vibration is to reminding you of who you really are

Thank you, for sharing your light on this topic. I am sure this is a blessing to many who will find or understand at least the meaning of their journey here now.

There are many spiritual laws that we have not mentioned here, but as Emanual says, you will draw the law to you that you are ready to receive or are ready to learn at exactly the right time in your life. Here are a few that I feel we could all use at this point in time:

You hold the keys to your own destiny.

Only you can unlock what lies within.

Trust in the process.

Trust in you.

Find love in your heart, and be the love to others.

Be the guiding light that shines within,

and unite with the universal wisdom of source.

I am guiding you and teaching you to
recognise your life's experiences and to
learn from them to grow.

So, you can create essentially the life that
you are here to live.

CHAPTER SIX

LEARN TO LISTEN

Here on the Earth, I lived many lifetimes, child.

Over and over again,

I relived the same path.

I did not realize this was so.

Each of my journeys in life

I experienced as a man.

Each of my journeys were selfless and loveless.

I was full of bitterness and hatred.

I was full of the injustice that life had served me,

and I wanted vengeance.

It is here where our learning lies, child.

Life has not served this to you; you have created your own destiny, your own path.

Through your own thoughts and words that you think, feel, and speak.

You are responsible for your own words and actions.

You and only you can change the life you are here to live; you must take responsibility for your future actions and find forgiveness for all that has been and gone.

I encourage you and all of humanity to embrace this opportunity for change.

Welcome this opening of the heart and mind,

and be the joy, love and light that you are here to be.

Surround yourself with laughter, not bitterness.

Surround yourself with joy, not sadness.

Surround yourself with love, not hurt.

Surround yourself with experience, not regret.

And so, you see the pattern here that is unfolding.

Allow this flow of the universe to come to you.

As I am working with you now, child, I wish I had known of this when I was on the Earth, for my knowledge on the Earth was of God and the gods.

I especially worshiped Jupiter in our lifetime, as his strength and vigor was a match to my earthly life. I would pray to him to keep me safe and strong, to be with me on our campaigns, to fight and to bring honor and justice to my life.

The Romans worshiped many gods and goddesses. Through research, I found that the most important of them from the time that Emanuel speaks of during the Antonine Wall were as follows:

Jupiter was the most important of the Roman gods. He was often referred to as the king of the gods, the main ruler of heaven and earth, the wielder of thunder bolts and lightening. As he was the most celebrated god of ancient Rome, the Romans would call him *Jupiter Optimus Maximus*, meaning 'the best and the greatest'.

Minerva was the goddess of wisdom and war. It was thought that from the heavens she could oversee everything that would require careful thought or calculation. She brought intelligence and inspiration to her patrons and was renowned for her wisdom. She was often called upon before battle commenced to help give a clear plan and direction for the attack. Minerva is often pictured with her helmet, shield, and spear.

Ceres was the goddess of agriculture and the harvest, especially grain. It was believed that if you worshipped her, she would protect the new seeds as they were being sown and create a fertile land to ensure a full and ripe harvest for all. Ceres is often pictured in draping robes and with a basket full of fruit and flowers, sometimes wearing a garland made of corn.

Nemesis was the goddess of fortune. This fortune could be good or bad, depending on what the person deserved to receive. Nemesis either celebrated good deeds already done or handed out punishment for evil deeds or undeserved good fortune. A goddess not to be messed with. Nemesis is often pictured with the scales of justice to restore balance and justice to the earthly world.

Bonus Eventus was the god of good luck, success and happy outcomes. He was worshipped around business, financial and hopeful futures, especially in anything concerning money. He is often seen on Roman coins holding a libation bowl, which was used in prayer.

Apollo was the god of prophecy, or divine assistance, and presided over the universal laws. He was the most heavenly of all the gods. Apollo inspired music, poetry, and artistic creativity. Apollo also brought order to humankind and was a source of all medical knowledge. He was a giver of law and of healing. He is often pictured holding a golden bow.

The Romans would set up an altar as a place to meet with the gods in prayer; it was an opportunity to ask for help or forgiveness. Altars could also be set up for times of celebration. The names of the god that they would be praying to were often carved into the altar stones. These inscriptions can be seen on some of the altars that were erected along the Antonine Wall. The images of the gods were also sometimes inscribed onto rings with *intaglios* (carved gemstones).

If you had known that you had your own personal spirit guide back then, Emanuel, when you walked the Earth, would you have been conversing with him as I am with you now?

Ha ha!! You do make me laugh, child.

Yes, I believe I would have prayed with him, in preference to the gods, as I do not think that my acceptance of communication, as it were, would have allowed my strength of belief that this could be so.

So, you would not have believed this possible?

No, not at all.

Even though my lifetime here was about opening my mind and soul and accepting God into my heart.

I do not consider that this would have been an option for me here.

It has been on my ascension, my learning here in the hereafter of consciousness, that I now understand how the

laws of the universe work and how we are many who are assigned to help each one of you.

If you could go back to your earthly life now, Em, what advice would you give yourself now?

Be free.

Free from burden, grief, hatred, injustice, poverty,

and allow love and joy to flow freely through your heart.

Live life in joy.

Enjoy the experience of life,

and live each day as a new day full of opportunity and grace.

And do not be frightened to do so, do not let the words of others or other judgements prevent you from living wholeheartedly.

Be free to love, to be free, to be happy. Be free to live life in every moment.

How can I help you to inspire others to live and really embrace the opportunity to experience the joy in life and work with their own spiritual guides or mentors here, please?

We are all connected in a spiritual sense,

for we are all divine beings of God.

We are all connected to the universal wisdom of truth.

We are calling – are you listening? This question is of most importance here as

listening is the key to connection here, child.

The connection to the divine universe is for all to have –

You just need to know how to use it.

It is a bit like a dial-up phone call.

You lift the receiver and wait to be connected.

And if you are listening correctly, you will hear the person at the other end of the line.

I am laughing here now, child, at my own explanation of this, but it seems as simple as that.

How can we learn to listen, Emanuel?

Patience and stillness of the mind, child.

A few years ago, I attended a demonstration evening within a spiritualist church. I was invited to go along by a work colleague at the time. It was a newly formed church, and they had quite a few good events advertised. So, we decided to go along to see what it was all about.

On the first evening, there was a church service with a mediumship demonstration.

A mediumship demonstration, for those who may not be familiar with this, is where a medium delivers evidence-based communication from Spirit and loved ones to members of the audience.

We had arrived just in time as there were only two seats left at the very front of the hall. You could feel the excitement all around the room as everyone waited for the service to start.

The medium was sitting directly in front of me. I remember thinking he looked so young, and I noticed he was holding a clear crystal in one hand and was fidgeting away, as he was obviously sitting full of anticipation. As the service got underway, the young man introduced himself as David, and explained that this was his first platform demonstration, so he was a little nervous. As he started his demonstration of mediumship, boy, did he take us all by surprise. He was amazing, and the detailed information and validation that he gave to the members of the audience was astounding. There was a real buzz in the air. Just before the session ended, he asked if he could come to me, and of course I said yes. He passed me a very heart-warming message from my late mother. and as I was close to tears, he said, 'Do not leave the service until I have spoken to you at the end, please.' This took me a little by surprise, so, of course, I waited for a little longer at the end to see what he wanted to say to me.

He asked me if I had ever attended a spiritualist church or had sat in a development circle before. I said no and that this was all very new to me, and I certainly did not know what a development circle was. He said he was glad that I had come along as he felt that Spirit wanted to work with me. He explained that sitting in a circle was a way of learning to sit in meditation whilst strengthening up our skills for connecting to Spirit. I told him that I'd never heard of such a thing, and he laughed. He said, 'I do not want you to leave here tonight until I have introduced you to the church chairperson, as I really feel that you would benefit from attending a circle.' I was a bit confused as to what was going on, to be honest. But I was introduced to a few of the church members who were all very friendly and welcoming, and so it was that I was invited to go along and sit in their open circle to see how I got on.

Be still, be calm, be connected.

Be grounded to the earth and allow the soul to sing.

For here you will allow yourself to be open, to be free.

It is the opening of the heart and mind,

the trusting of God or the universal wisdom that surrounds you

that lifts the veil between us.

When I arrived for the first session, I could see that all the seats were laid out on a circle around the room. We were welcomed and told to sit where we felt drawn to.

I was a bit nervous as I looked around the room at all these new faces, but I figured as it was a new church, everyone else was new here, too.

It was clearly explained to us that regular meditation practice can help us to focus on the energy centers within our own body and help us learn how to feel this energy. We also learned how to then build upon or expand this energy, otherwise called 'raising your vibration'. By raising our vibration, we learn how to welcome our guides or spirit helpers and learn what their essence and energy feels like. This way, we learn to allow them to work with us, developing our skills towards becoming working mediums.

This is an especially important part of our spiritual development, and by building on this through regular practice, we will learn and allow the other world to work with us. By calming the mind, we are becoming open or receptive to the energies that surround us, attuning ourselves to how they feel.

Here is the meditation that we were guided on:

Sit in a comfortable position.

And relax, relax the body and mind.

Take a deep breath in for a count of four.

Hold for a count of four.

And release for a count of four.

As you breathe in, use the in-breath to sweep up anything that you have accumulated throughout the day that no longer serves you, and as you breathe out, let it all go. Let go of all the stress and strains of the day and welcome this inner calm.

Allow yourself to let go.

Surrender to the moment of calm.

Allow the journey of stillness to surround you.

If your mind starts to wander, just let your thoughts go and come back to the breathing again until you settle into this rhythm of breath which allows you to drift off into a stillness of the mind.

As we learn to do this practice, we are learning to be open, we are learning to be aware, and we are learning to listen. We are connecting to the soul.

Connecting to the soul, yes, I like this description here, child,

for you are connecting to the essence of you, who you really are.

And you will build upon this energy, this thought, this

intention, with an opening of your heart.

The feeling of expansion in this way is a feeling of the divine or unconditional love.

This is an important part of my teachings here, child, for if we can help others to achieve this and make the connection, they will in turn learn to connect with their own guides or spiritual helpers as we are today.

Energy follows thought, so a strong intention of connection is also required here, child.

Set your intention.

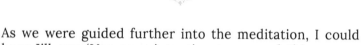

As we were guided further into the meditation, I could hear Jill say, 'Use your intention to expand this energy outside of your bodies. Allow the energy to grow as far as you possibly can.'

As we were all brought back from our meditation journey, there was such a lovely calm feeling all around the room; everyone looked surreal and happy to have shared in this little exercise.

This was the first of many outings to the open circle, as they were held every Saturday after the main church service. As everyone there was new, it was a real bonding of friendship that grew among us, all kindred spirits, welcoming this learning experience with Spirit.

Brotherhood, child, a coming together of souls for the purpose of spiritual growth.

Was that my purpose for attending the church, Em, to learn how to listen?

Yes, that among other things, child, for you had many opportunities to work with us, but you chose to avoid them.

This is true, Emanuel; I did have some very strange experiences when I was a child. I would hear whispers at night, as I was trying to get to sleep, and I would hide under the duvet, so I could not hear them. I would hear my name being called. This gave me so much fear that I did not want to listen!!

This was not entirely your own fault here, for you did not have the knowledge of understanding that was required to undertake this journey. So, we directed you onto this path of learning through the church once we felt you were ready, as it would build your own trust in Spirit. For you to build trust in yourself, to give you the confidence and the knowledge and understanding of how we communicate with you, and to guide you into being able to share this gift to others.

This is my gift to you.

This is my gift to humanity.

This is my gift to all the souls that are lost and searching for the new.

This is my purpose, to help you teach and grow with a strong faith in the divine.

Let it flow.

I see it for myself here, as Emanuel says – listening is the most important thing we can learn to do.

Not only for our connection to Spirit but also for our connection to people. Learning to listen is a gift. Take a moment here to just listen to the sounds that are around you now:

The cars outside driving past your window.

The wind blowing through the trees.

Your neighbour's tv, which might be too loud.

The gentleness of the birds singing.

Whatever surrounds you now.

Just sit still in this moment and listen.

Regular meditation practice is the best way to strengthen your communication to Spirit. There are some great guided meditations out there, and I would suggest trying out quite a few different techniques until you see which one sits with you.

Spirit-guided meditations will be the most powerful, child, and please, now let me lead the way with this.

Be calm in the moment.

Be still in the moment.

Be comfortable in your pose.

Settle your posture,

and let your eyes close.

Allow the calmness to settle on your shoulders.

Take a long slow breath in, to fill the chest and lungs, and as you do, say, 'I am opening my heart to love.'

And as you slowly breathe out, say, 'I am letting go of all that I no longer need.'

Please repeat this three times.

Observing your breath, observing the body,

notice any areas of the body where you are holding onto tension.

Take some time to focus here and it let go.

Relax the head, the neck and shoulders,

as we move down through the body,

into your arms, your chest, and breathe.

Slowly release as we move further through the body,

Down through your chest, the tummy, the hips.

Sense anywhere that we are letting go of all tension,

down through your legs and feet,

until you are now feeling truly relaxed.

As you expand your attention out with your body and into the stillness,

listen to the sounds that are here.

Listen, not just with your ears but with your whole awareness, your aura, your light.

Hear how close these words are to you now.

Hear the sounds that are in the room and the space that you are in.

Listen to the space between the sounds, the silence,

expanding your awareness again to include the more distant sounds outside,

being receptive and open to the most distant sounds that you can receive.

Sensing the balance,

relaxing into to this space of listening,

notice how you recognize these sounds by your awareness.

As each sound appears, acknowledge them and let them go,

as though they were clouds passing in the sky

with gentle, effortless movement.

Allow your inner thoughts to flow from you

as you are receiving.

Rest in this awareness, be still in the calmness that surrounds you now.

This is your home,

completely in the stillness of love.

And when you are ready, take a slow and steady breath.

Bring yourself back to center,

rooted and grounded to the Earth.

Give blessings for what has been.

Honor the essence of what is here and around you in this moment.

And so, it is.

Allow your meditation practice to become your listening practice, not only for the outside world, but for a way to strengthen your listening to the self.

Each session does not need to be long-winded or extensive for your learning. But each session should become a part of your daily practice to heal your heart within.

Enjoy it, embrace it, be thankful.

Be free.

Free from burden, grief, hatred, injustice,
poverty, and allow love and joy to flow
freely through your heart.

Live life in joy.

Enjoy the experience of life, and live each
day as a new day full of opportunity and
grace.

Chapter Seven

Past Lives and Insights

Can you tell me more about who I was in this past life, please?

Yes, child.

I wondered when you would get around to asking this question.

You were my friend.

My dear friend.

You, too, were a warrior of faith.

But as I had vengeance in my heart,

you only had love.

I had never known anyone with such forgiveness within.

You were my inspiration, my healing, my light.

I was proud to serve beside you, as your brother in arms.

My fight was for vengeance.

Your fight was for honour, dignity, and respect.

And as such, we had the upmost admiration for you.

And who you were.

In a way, we have swapped roles here,

as you taught me how to forgive in life,

how to love those around me.

We had a strong bond of faith,

in the faith of what was to become.

You showed me the way to God,

how to pray, how to heal, how to grow.

These things I will never forget.

And I thank you.

I thank you, Emanuel, for sharing in these wonderful insights into my past life

If I guided you, in all of these things, then who was I?

You were the son of a great leader.

You were born to become the role you played.

Are you saying here that I had been born into an important family?

Yes, in a way. But not of great wealth or stature. Your family was very honourable; they stood by their word. Your father was trusted by many men, and he brought you up to have the same values as he did. These values led to opportunity which, in turn, led him to become a leader. And you would follow in his footsteps as you became older.

Your agenda in life was set out for you from an incredibly young age. Your parents taught you about God and to have faith in the divine; they were your inspiration. Your father taught you how to fight, and how to be brave. He believed in you.

Once your father died, you, too, took the lead, and led many men into battle.

I have such a proudness in my heart as I recount this memory.

I was proud of you then; I am still proud of you today.

Truth honour Integrity – these are the words of wisdom you shared with us, as I share with you now.

What do you mean by these words, Emanuel? What do truth, honour and integrity mean to you?

You used these words to touch our hearts, to give us strength to fight and to remind us that we were at one with God or the god that we called upon in that moment.

I am here to remind you now of these words, I am calling you back to these wordsnow, as I ask you to use them again in this lifetime with the same vigour and courage as you did then. Now, rise as if you were leading us into battle again. To stand up and be seen and to charge forward in this lifetime with faith in our hearts, lead the way and we will follow.

Living and speaking in truth, child, is a consistency within the mind; it is your will and your trait, your courage. Truth is an expression of God. It is a fact of belief that is accepted as so. Use it to heal the hearts of others.

Honour reminds us of who we really are, and how we should treat one another. How we should work in honour together to help bring out the best in others. Honour helps us to believe in ourselves and to believe in those around us. To see in oneself what others shall bring. Honour brings people together as they recognize something within themselves is worth aiming for.

Integrity allows us to know the truth and live by it. It is our honesty and our fairness. Our spiritual integrity is about making choices that are for our greatest and highest good and aligning choices to be our most beautiful and divine self. Our oneness with God. We will be helping others to understand divinity.

Be the creator of your own destiny; write your own story in life.

Do not follow others in grief or pain.

Create your life, create your love, and share it.

You have lived many lifetimes here now, child.

For your path has been long, just as mine.

You are now, I believe as they say, an old soul.

You were a great warrior,

and now you are here, shining your light for God

to lead this way forward.

How do I lead in this way that you ask?

Listen, always listen

and ask.

What should I ask?

'What are you trying to show me?'

Really! As simple as that?

As simple as that. Ask to see the signs, then look for the signs, the signals that have been placed all along your life journey so far.

They are all there.

You just need to take the time to look back and source them out.

The experiences in your life that have stayed with you, memories that have a significant theme –

these are your signposts or life signals pointing you along your way.

Ok, on that note, I thought I should again heed the words Emanuel had shared here.

I sat down with a pen and paper, and I began creating a list all of the things that stood out to me throughout my own life. By this, I mean listing my life experiences, the vibrant ones that stood out. I was looking for the signposts, the flags of colour that really grabbed my attention, just as Emanuel had suggested.

I wrote at the top of a piece of paper, 'What is my most memorable life experience?'

Then, I asked out loud, just as Emanuel had advised – 'What are you trying to tell me?'

All of a sudden, a memory came flooding back to me. It was something that I had not thought about for years, which really took me by surprise. It was a memory of my Primary 7 school trip where we all went to Hadrian's Wall and Northumberland National Park; I must have only been about age 12 or 13 at the time.

Hadrian's Wall is the most famous of all the frontiers of the Roman Empire. It was built to guard the wild northwest frontier of the Roman Empire for nearly 300 years. It was built by the Roman army on the orders of the Emperor Hadrian following his visit to Britain in 122 AD. It is 84 miles in length from coast to coast, starting at Wallsend on the River Tyne, crossing through the Northumbrian countryside, passing through Carlisle and finishing on the Solway coast, with the Scottish hills in the distance.

The wall was built by 15,000 men in less than six years, an outstanding accomplishment of engineering, its purpose to separate the barbarians from the Romans.

Once we arrived and descended from our school bus, we were welcomed into the hostel which would be our base and accommodation for the next few days. The teachers did a quick head count to see if we were all there, and we were directed to our dormitory.

After a quick meeting with our teachers, we were all keen to go out and experience our surroundings. We were handed a copy of itinerary for the next few days, so we could all see exactly what we were going to be doing and where we would be going. I remember being really excited about the trip as I had never been away from home on my own in a large group or with my friends before. However, as being an early teenager at the time, I couldn't really show how excited I was to my peers – that would have been just a bit too uncool, especially as were here on the topic of history.

We set out to enjoy the remainder of our first day. Firstly, we learned that in its time, Hadrian's Wall had been a rich and vibrant place. It was a border created for the Romans; it was also a place where borders were crossed, as a coming together of many. It was here that soldiers and civilians from across Europe and North Africa met. Many people traded goods and served together. Civilians would settle here, making it their home. As such, this would make them interested in adopting local customs, alongside learning to worship native gods, creating a learning experience of the new, whilst keeping some of their own country's beliefs and traditions. This was a new and growing community in which even rebels could become allies and lifelong friendships were made. .an

On our second day, we set off to visit Houseteads Fort, which is on the line of Hadrian's Wall. I clearly remember the starting point for the wall was from the car park leading up to the site. We were in a school class of around 25 children and were instructed by our class teacher to walk beside one another in pairs. For a little fun and to get into the swing of the theme here, our teacher suggested that we start to march, just like the Roman soldiers would have done whilst walking along this same stretch of ground. After our opportunity to walk part of the wall, we headed to the museum, which had both an outdoor site with ongoing excavation and an indoor Roman army museum full of interesting artifacts and treasures; there was so much to see and learn.

When we arrived at Housteads, I remember saying to my friend, 'I think I have been here before.'

She asked me, 'Why?' And I remember saying, 'I don't actually know, but I know that I have.' I actually felt quite overwhelmed, and I fainted at one point of the day, too. The teacher put this down to dehydration from the travel. Now that I am revisiting this experience, I think I was overwhelmed from the vibration of energy that surrounded me.

On the last day, we were to visit the Brocolitia Roman Temple so we could learn about the various Roman religious practices. The Brocolitia temple is dedicated to Mithras, the god of light. It is believed that the romans celebrated Mithras on the 25th of December, interestingly, the same day that Christians have chosen to celebrate the birth of Christ.

Mithras is also known as the god of the rising sun; he oversaw the orderly change of the seasons and was responsible for bestowing divine grace. He was a protector to the faithful, also known as the god of war, and as such he was invoked by warriors before battle. The temple here was created in the 3rd century, so quite some time after myself and Emanuel would have been there.

Before we knew it, the three-day trip had passed us by, and we were back on the bus to head home. The first thing that I asked my mum when I saw her was, 'Have we been Hadrian's Wall before?"

And, of course, the answer was NO. My mother said that she had never even been there herself. So, I dismissed my idea of having been there befor and settled with the dehydration story for my lightheadedness, as the teacher had suggested. I had never given this event another moment of thought until now!

The Romans stayed at Hadrian's Wall until around 140 AD when they moved north to the Antonine Wall.

Did we stay at Hadrian's Wall, Emanuel?

Yes, you did, for many years. Your life was here for the most part of it. And so, your inner knowing from your school trip was correct at the time. A timely event connecting you to your intuition.

We, of course, met once you moved across to the Westerwood fort at the Antonine Wall, as I have described in the first of our chapters.

How old were you when you died, Emanuel?

In this lifetime that we speak of here, I was age 42. You, however, lived a few years longer, until the age of 46.

That's funny as I am 46 now.

Yes, and this is no coincidence. In this current lifetime, you have chosen to experience what it would be like to live longer than your 46th year. As in this past life, you had already experienced such victory. Your desire now for this lifetime is to seek out what more you could possibly achieve in a life beyond your 46th year, what other great battles you could overcome and how you could continue to lead and inspire others to do so. You also wanted to come back to share with others the simplest of attributes such as kindness, humility, compassion and love.

Can you bring some of your previous life experiences or even memories with you from your past life into this next life?

Yes, of course.

Remember, we are divinely connected.

However, once your soul reincarnates, you will arrive in your earthly body and very rarely remember the details from your past lives. You will have a different name, personality, and body. However, the soul has travelled for many lifetimes with you, and it is here that you may bring forward experiences from a previous lifetime.

You will not know what this lifetime has planned for you.

Often, you will experience all the hardships of life before you reach your true spiritual self or, should I say, before life leads you onto your spiritual path.

Through my research, I found out that children are most likely to remember their past lives, and memories of this may appear between the ages of 2-4 and may show up as behaviours or associated phobias. Past-life memories can also show up as recurring dreams. There are ways in which these memories can be retrieved, with the help of treatments such as past-life progression therapy, but your focus is to live in the here and now.

When you stumble across these recollections, you're the bridge between the two worlds. It will feel like meeting an old friend. And although you may not remember the how's, whys or where's of the experience, you will have an overwhelming feeling or inner knowing – just as I had felt at Hadrian's Wall.

Focus on the familiar.

The trusting, the knowing is the beginning.

We have all come to the Earth to experience life.

Please note my word 'experience'.

You gain this experience by observing and participating or taking part in everyday life. This is how we are constantly obtaining knowledge, through doing, seeing, and feeling.

You are here to live, you are here to be.

Use your experiences to learn and grow from.

Take your negative experiences and turn them into a positive experience, in which you can help or share with another how to heal, expand and grow.

Take your positive experiences and multiply them.

We are all on the path to ascension.

Live the life you are here to experience.

Become the person you are meant to be.

This message is not just for you, Jacqueline, this message is for you to learn from and help to send it our around the world to everyone, everyone who is ready to hear it.

Those who are not ready to live and breathe in their divine spirituality will not hear you.

Those who are ready and awakening will not only hear you, they will have heard their own calling. They will see you and through your spoken word, you will help to shine the light of the divine into their hearts.

We are healing.

The world is changing.

We are learning.

Be giving.

Be kind.

Show love.

Show compassion.

Be grateful.

Be forgiving.

Be thankful.

These are all the gifts you have brought with you for your journey through life. Use them well. I do not say this only to you, child, for humanity as a whole has forgotten how to use them. These attributes of the self are gifts from the universe for you to use and share with others.

This message that I am here to share is to remind you and

each and every one of you.

Once you remember who you are, who you truly are as a divine soul, when you embrace this thought, and once again start to welcome these selfless acts of gratitude and kindness into your daily life, this is when your life will change, and Change for the better.

Humanity as a whole will change.

The world will change,

and the world we live in will change

all for the better.

This message is to be shared and passed on, it is like the links of a chain.

One by one, we will relink and connect to the universal energy,

strengthen our beliefs,

for our greatest and higher good,

so that once again we can be proud of the world that we live in.

Not only for today, but for the future.

Your future.

We are healing.

The world is changing.

We are learning.

Be giving.

Be kind.

Show love.

Show compassion.

Be grateful.

Be forgiving.

Be thankful.

CHAPTER EIGHT

SPIRITUAL AWAKENING

We are here to work together.

Your own spirit guides, ancestors and angels are here to help you.

It is time to overcome fear.

It is time to overcome negativity.

It is time to be you.

Step into the new joy of life.

How can we do this, Emanuel?

Let go of any beliefs that are holding you back in life.

As your guide and as all guides we are watching over your daily struggles,

we wish to ask you all of you to now stand in your power.

Reinstate your self-belief.

There is so much negativity which surrounds humanity.

This is a time for healing,

a time for growing

and a time for expansion.

A true spiritual awakening

for all.

Believe in yourself for you are a divine being of light,

and you are a gracious spirit of God.

Shine now, shine.

Touch the hearts of all those around you

to reveal your greatest purpose.

This is where your life begins in abundance.

When you look into your past, you will see the path to your future.

The synchronicities of life are entwined with the universe.

They all lead to the plan of your soul.

Look for the way.

We are calling.

As Emanuel said that the divine universe is calling us now, I wanted to research some information on how we can recognise the signs of our own spiritual awakening. I know that I felt my calling as I was asked to write this book, and I wanted to share with you some ways in which you may feel your own calling, too.

I have placed my findings here into small categories to make it as simple as possible for each of us to recognise and act on.

What follows are the seven stages of our spiritual awakening as I understand them to be.

1 BEGIN

The beginning. Each and every one of us are on a journey through life, whether we choose to recognise it or not. We will not know in advance what our pre-planned journey holds for us, but at some point, we will become more aware that there is something more than just us. And so, we begin to align to our true purpose and our life synchronicities begin. We may stumble upon a spiritual book or hear a friend talking about angels as a gentle introduction to the idea that life is not just an everyday experience. We are actually divine beings who are here to learn, grow and become.

2 RECOGNISE

We are all going through the motions of our daily lives, and often we have the feeling of just trying to fit in. Once we are ready to recognise that we don't really fit in, but we still don't want to stand out from the crowd, this is when we are ready to recognise our inner being. Sometimes we need a nudge to get us to move beyond this point; often this is when things will happen in our personal lives such as a crisis, trauma, or bereavement. Something so life changing that it will take us to the depths of despair, our breaking down of reality, so that we have nowhere else to turn but to God, the divine, our angels or spirit guides. This is a strengthening of our beliefs.

3 SEARCH

Once we have reached our lowest breaking point or crisis point in our lives, we often feel like we are searching, we are looking, looking for something more. It is here that our daily lives may feel like they have lost their meaning, and we have lost the ability to see the joy that surrounds us. Once we are here in this painful and sometimes traumatic stage, we will often suffer depression, anxiety, lack of sleep or hold an unknown deep sadness within.

This is an important and necessary stage of our awakening. Unfortunately, if you do not recognise why this is happening to you, you can, of course, choose to stay in this cycle of repeating patterns. This is where we are looking to blame others to avoid our own personal responsibility. We are holding onto our limiting beliefs and holding ourselves back

Some of our limiting beliefs are:

I'm not good enough

I'm the victim

I can't do it

I don't deserve to be

I'm not clever enough

I'm not enough.

4 TRUST

As we are building a trust in the divine, we start to get stronger within ourselves. We have the courage to seek the new. We are willing to take responsibility for our actions and are no longer willing to repeat the old; we are breaking away from our old habits. This is the new you, standing in your power of belief.

5 INSIGHT

Full of new insight and excitement, we are willing to learn new ways of turning our life experiences into opportunities. We are willing to be open to the possibilities of spiritual guidance, and we are gaining lots of knowledge through reading books and by attending courses or workshops. We are open-minded and willing to let go of all that no longer serves us. Our friendship groups or relationships may be changing at this point; we are attracting the right new people and circumstances into our lives as we are realigning to our true selves. Happiness has returned within.

6 GROWING

We are growing at a rapid rate here and have found a new enthusiasm for life. We are letting go of all our doubts and insecurities and are happy within ourselves. We are in awe of the limitless knowledge and growth we have found, and we will want to share this with others. We are surrounded with love, joy and happiness as we have opened our hearts to receive, and we are in the flow of the Universal abundance

7 UNDERSTANDING

We have the greatest understanding of spiritual wisdom, we are acknowledging a greater being within us and our extension to God, the Universal wisdom, consciousness. We welcome this inner knowing with acceptance from our heart and mind. We are divine

We are expanding as the spiritual beings we are here to be and, once again, and becoming true to ourselves.

Can this happen to anyone, Emanuel?

Yes, of course, this is possible for all.

It may, of course, take a few lifetimes to recognise what you are doing here.

I would say that new souls may take at least two lifetimes before they feel their reconnection to Spirit.

Their first bodily experience of humanity is in the forefront

and as our learning is primarily what we are here for, you will, of course, experience this first.

No matter what lifetime you are in, you will live out your life experiences first to lead you on your way to enlightenment.

Is there anything else we should be doing to help us recognise our own awakening?

Just trust in the process.

It all happens in divine timing,

the synchronicities of your life.

You do not need to hold worry, stress, and sadness in your life.

You only need to welcome joy, love, and happiness,

and share this for all.

What you give, you will receive.

Financial burdens or freedom are not necessities for life.

However, the abundance of the universe will flow to those who are ready to receive it.

Once we are ready to receive, what should we do?

There is nothing that you need to do.

You just need to believe that it will be so.

How can we help others to connect to their own spirit guides, just like you?

There are many ways to connect to the divine, and not everyone will be ready to communicate directly. However, I believe that a good starting point would be to welcome into your life crystals from the Earth.

Crystals for connection?

Yes, align with the crystals of the Earth child for these are incredible manifestations of light that will help you with your purpose.

Crystals can help align the energies and raise the vibration for a faster and smoother connection to Spirit.

They will also help keep you grounded into every essence of your being.

As much as I love crystals myself, I had never considered them a tool for connecting with the divine.

Surely, we need more than just some crystals to connect?

Yes, of course.

Connection is all about your intention.

But for a beginner who does not yet fully trust in themselves,

by adding in the Earth here, it adds a little extra magic.

I like your description here, Emanuel. How do we know which ones we need?

You will feel the energetic pull from the crystal; it will draw you to it. As such, the crystal will choose you, rather than you choosing it.

And with that, I was off again, researching all that I could find on crystals for spiritual connection. There are so many to choose from. I have included the ones here which I found to be the most popular and powerful when working with spirit guides or our ancestors. I also found that the Romans would use different types of crystals as amulets and talismans. This was very common amongst the Roman soldiers, who often carried the tiger's eye stone to provide protection in battle. Roman crystals were also used in medical treatment to enhance their health and to attract desirable things.

My research allows me to share with you some of the most popular crystals for connection to the spirit realm. I hope by sharing these few findings that I may inspire you to start your own little collection of gemstones.

JADE

Colour – deep green

Jade can be used to contact your ancestor spirits. Many people believe jade helps heal karma in your ancestral line. As your connection to your ancestors is very important, going back and healing things that are passed down in your family lineage is a powerful practice; jade can help with this.

ANGELITE

Colour – soft blue

This crystal can help you connect with your spirit guides and angels. It brings the protective energy of your guides into your space. Angelite can help you find a great deal of comfort, keeping you feeling safe and supported. It is excellent for stimulating your intuition and allowing messages from your guides to come through, loud and clear. This is one of my personal favourites.

GREEN AVENTURINE

Colour – soft green

This crystal promotes harmony in your environment, especially in your sacred space. When working with spiritual beings, it's helpful to make sure that your space is calm, tranquil and free from psychic debris. Green aventurine works to keep things peaceful and harmonious so that communication continues in a positive, progressive manner.

MALACHITE

Colour – deep green

Malachite invites protective guides into your space to watch over you and all members of your family. This crystal can be placed near the door so that anyone entering your home will be protected while they're within that energy. It also helps you communicate with spirits that seem to be stuck in a space, keeping you protected before and after contact.

SCOLECITE

Colour – soft white

Scolecite is an ascension stone that helps you connect to your higher self. This stone is a high vibrational stone, which makes it excellent for connecting with our ancestors, angels and spirit guides.

When working these crystals, it is recommended to make sure you also have grounding and protection crystals, such as hematite or black tourmaline.

Is there anything else you would like to add here, Emanuel?

Yes, *flower essences.*

Really? So, now I think I have gone mad. You would like me to add flower essences here?

Yes, why do you doubt it?

You are all at one with the Earth.

The earth is at one with the divine source of eternal life.

We have worked with these essences for many lifetimes,

and will continue to do so for many more.

These will make powerful remedies for healing

and align you to your soul.

Again, I was off for some further research on the topic of flower essences and essential oils. From my findings, here are just some of the most frequently used essential oils suggested to promote our spiritual awakening.

FRANKINCENSE

Helps assists us in the opening the third eye and getting in touch with our intuition. It is also a protector, shielding us from negativity. It is the perfect choice to help us alleviate stress or worry so that we can focus on our inner work. It invites us to release lower vibrations and reveals our inner truth.

ROSEMARY

Rosemary is often called the oil of knowledge and transition.

When we are doing inner work, we are constantly shifting and changing. Rosemary brings us comfort and support.

It helps with developing true knowledge of the self and brings us deeper into our soul purpose. It helps us ask those hard questions to really dig into answers that will move us along our path.

It invites us to trust in a higher vibration or power and feel supported during our work.

LAVENDER

Lavender brings us calm. It works well to help quiet our thoughts and allows us to open up during any spiritual work. When we use it for meditation, it helps us to connect to an even deeper level and allows us to get into our flow with ease.

ROMAN CHAMOMILE (I was so happy to see this one, and very apt for our topic, I thought!)

Roman Chamomile is a great oil for spiritual work as it allows us to see our true purpose. It helps us reveal our true nature and what we came to this earth to do.

This oil can help us release what no longer serves us and quit activities that are not furthering our purpose. It is a gentle reminder of why we are here and supports our true goal.

The Romans also loved herbs and are famous for their herb gardens, so here are some of the ways in which they were also used.

BAY – *Laurus nobilis*

A sacred herb for Apollo, the Greek god of prophecy.

It was also regarded as a symbol of victory by the Romans.

Bay was also used as a symbol of peace and would be passed between enemies when the battles were over.

ROSEMARY – *Rosmarinus officinalis*

Introduced into Britain by the Romans.

It was often pleated into crowns and garlands as it was thought to give the wearer great intelligence and memory.

THYME – *Thymus vulgaris*

Again, was introduced to Britain by the Romans.

The oil was used for massage therapy and was added to the bath water to increase vigour.

Thyme was also thought to be a good antidote for snake bites.

CARAWAY – *Carum carvi*

It was thought that the seeds could be chewed to relieve flatulence and indigestion.

Through history Julius Caesar referred to *chara*. This was a bread made from the caraway root and was mixed with milk

FENNEL – *Foeniculum vulgare*

Was used to give gladiators strength and stamina.

The dried leaves and seeds would be used to cure eye infections and inflammation.

Fennel seeds were also thought to stave off hunger.

HAWTHORN – *Crataegus monogyna*

In the language of flowers, hawthorn means hope.

Hawthorn crowns were often made and worn by brides.

Romans would place the leaves from the hawthorn plant in the hands of new babies for luck.

There are so many beautiful ways you can use your herbs or oils to support your journey. Oils may be diffused by using a gentle oil burner or steamer before or during meditation, journaling, or other spiritual practice.

You can apply them to the body, such as on the third eye or other chakra points, pulse points, or back of neck.

I hope this little exploration of these will inspire you to go deeper and try some for yourself!

Would you like to add anything further here, Emanuel?

Humanity as whole needs to remember the Earth, how important she is for your daily life.

She is always giving.

In your natural world – air, water, food, plants for medicine, shelter – she provides us with everything we need to survive.

Show her kindness and return her love, for the Earth provides you with many things and has done so for many generations.

The Earth's elements have many benefits – Earth, fire, water and wind.

Connect with these to connect to yourself.

Be at one with all of life and grow together.

Emanuel, are you talking about the five spiritual elements of the Earth here?

Earth, Fire, Water, Wind and Spirit

Earth grounds us to the earth and gives us strength and stability.

Fire is the element of love, warmth, compassion and connections to the heart.

Water represents our emotions it helps to keep us calm and allows the constant change and flow in our lives.

Wind brings us clarity and thought, the flow of new beginnings.

Spirit, sometimes called the fifth element, is the connection and balance for all the other elements to exist.

Yes, be respectful to the elements as they are respectful to you.

They will always be with you, within you and around you.

Take some time to appreciate them within.

Connect again to the power of the Earth to strengthen your connection to Spirit, divine consciousness, for it is all that is.

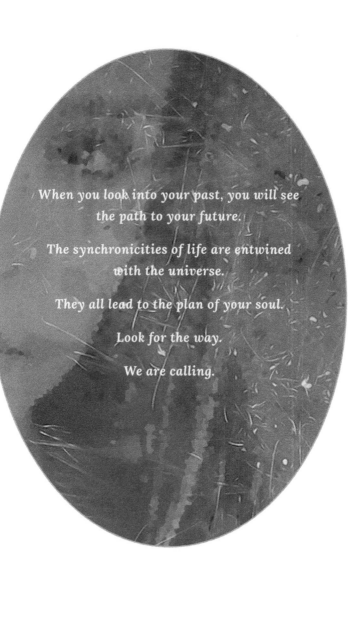

When you look into your past, you will see
the path to your future.

The synchronicities of life are entwined
with the universe.

They all lead to the plan of your soul.

Look for the way.

We are calling.

Chapter Nine

Our Soul Plan

Emanuel, when I knew that I would write this book, I found myself directed to have a soul plan reading session. Was this another of my pre-planned lessons?

Ahhh yes, child. You are now starting to truly recognize the twists and turns of fate and destiny in our lives. This pleases me greatly; you are learning.

During the first lockdown, I began to set up my own spiritual practice, as I mentioned earlier. I had started to do a daily meditation practice and was really focused on my connection with Spirit. I had spent several years sitting in a development circle for mediumship through my local spiritualist church; with this, I now felt ready to start offering one-to-one mediumship readings, and I was looking for different ways to grow my audience.

My cousin Leoni suggested to me that I should start following a business coach called Senga Cree on social media. Lianne explained that she had worked alongside Senga previously and knew that her inspiring coaching sessions would be right up my street, as she had a positive vibe and was very spiritually minded. Senga especially worked with woman to help them follow their dreams, and I liked the sound of this. I gratefully took my cousin's advice and started following the Woman Rising business page.

Within just a few weeks of following this amazing lady, I had signed up for a mini course that Senga offered called

'Money, Mindset, and Magic'. It sounded like the perfect dose of positivity needed for the lockdown situation we were in at the time, so I couldn't wait to get started.

The focus was all around positive intention and creating the mindset and magic that you would like to attract abundance into your life. By the end of the course, we had scheduled a one-to-one call to touch base and see where we could work together to build my own business to get the best possible results.

During our conversation, I explained that I was a spiritual medium and I felt I had been called to work in spiritual light. Immediately Senga said, 'Oh my goodness, you need to book a session with Sharyn. She will be able to help you immensely.' I had no idea who this lady was, but it sounded extremely exciting, so I asked for the details to get in touch with her to book a session.

This is where the amazing power of the internet comes in, as Sharyn turned out to be in South Africa!!

I sent a message via messenger, which said, 'Hi Sharyn, I got your details from Senga, and she suggested that I book a session with you?'

Little did I know that this session was about to change my life.

At this point, I still did not really know what sort of session I was booking, but I was trusting that this was meant for me.

Sharyn messaged to say that she would be delighted to book a session for me and asked if I could provide her with my birth name and date of birth. The session would be based on numerology and my soul plan. Up to this point, I had never heard of a soul plan before.

Our session was scheduled for a week later through a Zoom call. Sharyn had the most beautiful energy surrounding her when I first saw her through the screen. I was welcomed in the most gracious and warm way that you could have imagined. Straight away, Sharyn said that she was so excited to be speaking with me, and that she could not wait to share the details of my reading.

Sharyn explained that with my date of birth, she had been able to set out my life plan journey for this lifetime and this would explain what I was doing here and what I was here to learn.

The vibrancy and excitement from her energy was so contagious that I felt as though I were on cloud nine.

As we got started, Sharyn explained how amazing my mission and divine assignment was, and that it had been placed in no other heart but my own. With these words, I felt quite emotional before we had even begun.

Sharyn began with saying, 'It is time for you to step up and own your power and believe in yourself.'

I thought that was funny as I had written a remarkably similar statement from Emanuel earlier in my journal.

She continued, 'The vibrations from your birth name create the following meanings:

Your first name – Jacqueline – creates the vibrations for "spiritual warrior".'

The word warrior here made me smile, as Emanuel said we were warriors together, so already I was finding this interesting.

Sharyn continued to explain, 'You are an explorer of magic, looking for the light in everything. You have the gift of intuition. You are a pure channel for the divine. You are a teacher of courage to others, showing them how not to let the darkness stop them from shining their light out into the world. You are here to be an inspired messenger, teacher, and spiritual researcher.'

This statement I have found remarkably interesting, as I have recently had this conversation with my publisher. I believe my role in authoring this book has been in the form of a spiritual researcher, as I spend my time consistently researching the details from the channelled information that Emanuel has shared with me to reaffirm the information.

Carrying on, Sharyn said, 'You were born to have faith/ trust/courage in yourself and then teach this to others. There is a lot of spiritual energy around you. Your Surname – Turner – creates the vibrations for "Christ consciousness" and "third eye vision". Meditating and journaling are important to you and your connection to Spirit.'

I couldn't believe the accuracy of these words; again, this made me smile.

'Your destiny is to achieve a higher state of consciousness and to teach others on how to achieve theirs. You will become a conduit for Universal wisdom and selfless service for the divine. You will need courage, strength, curiosity, and willingness to step into your purpose, but it is time to shine your light.'

Emanuel has used these words repeatedly throughout my journaling with him – 'Shine your light.'

'You are going to write a book, my darling, as I see you are called to share your guided words with others.'

At this point, although I knew I was going to write a book, I didn't actually know yet how it would come out.

Looking back, the session was candidly informative and gave so much more detailed and in-depth information than I have shared with you here. But, as Emanuel has said, we have all planned our journey before we get here.

And I am now realising this is so.

Emanuel, how did you put together this seamless synchronicity of being directed to Senga to then directed to Sharyn to learn about soul planning?

Smiling here, child, for this was cleverly aligned into your journey.

Giving you a final little push here, another little exercise to strengthen your trust,

and for you to take heed of these words and place them into inspired action.

This is what you have done now, and I am blessed to be guiding you.

I can only thank you as this was an amazing experience for me to share here. How can we use this experience to now help and guide others in this way, or into inspired action, as you say?

You will become the teacher.

What sort of teacher?

For life, to live life by the journey of the soul, as we have discussed, child. Each of you will be having experiences along your life path. How you choose to use them or look at them is, of course, your own divine will.

It is in your power and the power that is within each one of you to take charge of your life.

Let go of all negativities.

Let go of all sadness.

Let go of what no longer serves your purpose.

And harness the energy from these in another way,

to create a new and positive experience,

one in which to learn and grow from.

Open the door to opportunity,

and accept it as so.

Are you saying that we all can change our path?

Yes, the power lies within you.

All of you.

Allow it to flow.

Align with the true being of light you are here to be.

And live your life in Joy.

What do you mean by 'allow it to flow'?

The energy of light surrounds you, it is within you, each and every one of you.

Embrace it, hug it, hold it in your essence of faith, trust and belief,

and it will flow through you.

All you need to do is remember.

Remember who you are within,

a divine being of light.

You are sent here to shine joy through your heart and the hearts of others.

Allow it to flow through you and to you.

Believe in the true inner you once again.

Do you know what your own soul plan lessons were for this lifetime that we are referring to in this book?

Yes, of course, as I have learned now,

But I would not have known what they were when I was walking this path.

As you arrive on the Earth each time,

your memory has been cleared.

You are staring the new with each lifetime.

Only in very exceptional circumstances may the soul remember who they were before.

What would they be?

Our master teachers sometimes arrive again on the Earth with their previous soul life memories.

It is to quicken the journey for them, as it is their purpose,

so they can teach as much information as possible in such a short space of time,

or lifetime, as you call it.

Do we need to remember our previous lifetimes?

Not necessarily, child.

There is no need for you to already know what has been, but there is no reason why you couldn't try to remember.

You have already set out this journey with your spirit guides and your master guides.

You have reviewed the lifetimes you have already made.

You have identified the areas that you have yet to learn from.

And you have agreed your plan to progress along with these new experiences.

You have already taken the time to acknowledge all the unanswered questions or regrets you may have. You have already taken the opportunity to have a life review.

And with this, you can see the experiences you have yet to gain.

And so, you already know what to do.

This made me start to think about the lifetime that Emanuel said we shared, and although I don't doubt it, I was interested in finding out more here on the topic of how we can remember our past lives.

As it seems, we arrive here in this lifetime without knowing what lies ahead for us in our journey.

But as we have had previous lifetimes, some elements from these may travel through time with us as part of our soul. As so, there are ways we can remember our past lives through past life regression therapy.

Are there any benefits for us to remember our past lives, Emanuel?

This is a big question, my child.

It is almost like asking how long a piece of thread is.

In a way, your lifetimes are all intwined with your past, present, and future.

What defines you today is a reflection of your past; it is like a ripple across the pond.

Your past life may help you to heal if you are feeling disengaged with your earthly lifetime in the moment. You may take the wisdom you have acquired from the past to lead you onto the future.

But it is not necessary to do so. I believe that if you feel drawn to exploring this further, then the door of opportunity should reveal itself to you effortlessly.

You have arrived here with all the tools you need to guide you through this lifetime.

Use them well.

I genuinely wanted to understand this past, present, and future connection with a bit more depth to see if the benefits of looking into our past lives could really help us with move forward with our current life journey or not.

From my research, I found that having the ability to learn about our past lives can be a wonderful way to unlock our inner potential, which can have a long-lasting and profound effect on our inner healing on all levels – physical, emotional, and spiritual.

Although this is not for everyone, as Emanuel says, there are some benefits to past-life regression therapy.

Mental and emotional clearing – Past-life regression may help to release any stagnant energy blocks related to pains, fears, and phobias. Negative emotions can influence our beliefs that may manifest into recurring emotional, mental, or behavioural patterns.

Awaken your life's purpose – Learning of your past life can allow you to have a deeper understanding of yourself. This understanding can bring you an inner sense of peace and belonging and help you to understand your strengths and weaknesses. This will allow you to align into the present moment and allow your true life's purpose to unfold.

Help you to understand your challenges – Some of the life challenges that you are facing today still have roots in your past. Being able to identify with these can allow a real healing to begin, whether that be through letting go with forgiveness, love, or compassion. It brings an opportunity to share and identify with a willingness to change and call it forthright into the now.

Releasing pain – It is thought that deep-seated muscular pain can be linked to memories buried within as unhealed wounds or past-life traumas. Past-life regression may help to release the energy blockages surrounding these and allow the healing process to begin, releasing and relieving the symptoms from the body.

Unlock your wisdom – You are a vessel of wisdom; you have lifetimes of experience within you – you just need to learn how to release this into your daily life to help you in the here and now. This higher level of perception can be life-changing and bring about immense healing within.

Live in the moment – Realization of our past lives and where we have come from leads to a deeper knowing that the soul is eternal. This brings us into the realization that we are now allowing an increased level of awareness to surround us, which will help us to live in the moment, let go of the past, embrace the future, and embrace the present moment.

The information that we hold from our past lives seem so powerful, as learning about these can not only bring us mental and emotional peace, but it can release us from physical pain. Learning about our past lives can lead us on the path to a deep level of healing and inner wisdom, which in turn will help us to open our hearts to joy and fulfilment within. Sometimes, we need to look back to our past endeavours to let go of what no longer serves us, which allows us to move forward into the new. A time for new beginnings

Emanuel, as we are talking of past lives, can you remember your own date and time of birth?

In the lifetime that we are talking about here, when I walked the earth with you, then yes, I can share this with you.

I was born on 01 March as the sun shined over Athens at 06.59 am in the year 120AD.

My mother named me after the month I was born.

She was so proud to have delivered a son.

This was something to be proud of, child, a boy,

for this was a significant triumph for a family in this time.

There was much joy and laughter to come in the days that followed.

Thank you for sharing this, Emanuel.

I felt drawn to take the time to research the details for the month of March in relation to the Roman calendar, which was called *Martius*. So remarkably close to the birth name Emanuel had shared with me – Martikus.

As you say there was so much joy in the days that followed, can you explain more, please?

A celebration, child, for the joy that a new birth shall bring.

There is no difference in time here, for the rituals of the new are the same: a time of rest for the mother, followed by gifts of fresh flowers and wine.

A son brought stature and pride to the family name and a prayer of thanks would be given to the gods. A child would not be fully celebrated until the first birthday in this time; then an altar would be set for prayer and thanks. The full integration of the soul has begun, and the new life has now began living and growing into his or her purpose. Here is where the fullest of merrymaking would begin.

Joy and celebration for all, a time for family and friends to unite together.

This is what is happening in a sense around the world for you now, child,

a remembrance for the joy in what and who you know.

The good is being restored into the hearts of many, with a time to reflect on what is important in life and to recognise those who have helped contribute to it.

This awakening is also a remembering of love and kindness.

As we have been talking about birth here, child, it is almost similar to the rebirth of humanity. The new path that is unfolding all around the world for those who are ready to follow their inner light and receive it. The rebirth of strength, kindness and unity in all and for those who are proud enough to stand up and deliver or share in the words of God to those who need it most.

We again will be at one with one another.

We again will align to the Earth and her plight.

We will again be the soldiers of honour that the world needs right now,

and I bless you all to do so.

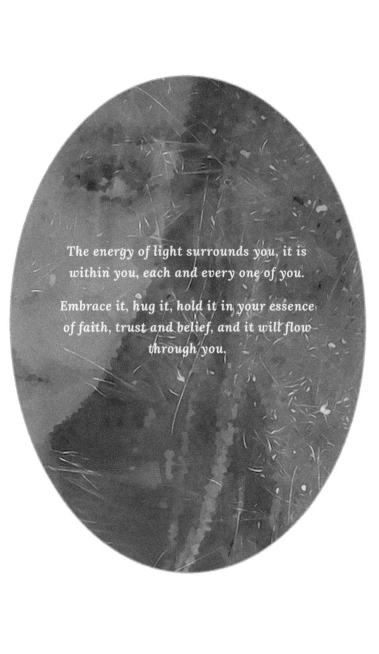

The energy of light surrounds you, it is
within you, each and every one of you.

Embrace it, hug it, hold it in your essence
of faith, trust and belief, and it will flow
through you.

Chapter Ten

So, what happens now, Emanuel?

I have given you the essential skills that you need to welcome Spirit into your life,

so that you can fully integrate into this new and evolving time.

Please take the time to read them, follow them and share them with everyone you shall meet.

You hold the gift of personal freedom. The choices that you make next are yours and yours alone.

I can only guide you.

This is a time of truth.

Step into courage, empowerment and compassion.

We are linking the bridge between the head, the heart, and the spiritual self,

and this, in turn, requires patience.

Spiritual ascension is not for the faint of heart here on the Earth.

It is a choice and a willingness to let go of the old and grow into your new.

It is a choice of living with heartfelt vision for the future, living in your truth.

There have been so many times during my journey with this book that I have asked myself:

Who am I?

Who am I to write this book?

Who am I to be sharing these words of wisdom?

Who am I to be seen in this way?

But it is my trust in Emanuel that pushes me forward each time with complete and utter faith in my heart.

I would like to take you back many years with me now and share one of my own important and touching writings from Emanuel. I want to highlight how it has helped me with my own trust whilst giving me strength in my belief that there is more out there and what we call the 'afterlife'.

I would like to accentuate the reality in which my writing with Emanuel has spanned over many years. We have covered several topics, filling up several journals. All the while, focusing on spiritual topics and advice not only for myself, but also, at times, for others.

In one of my early journals, dated 2010, the very first sentence from Emanuel still stands out to me so clearly now. His words are so precious to me and my current understanding that our path is already chosen.

I have chosen to share this writing not for the sadness that surrounds it, but in sharing the absolute wonder and sheer beauty of spiritual wisdom and what it can bring us. It shines a spotlight on our spirit guides and mentors. When we need them, they are there holding a vast valley of knowledge for what is already unfolding in our daily lives, in each moment of every day. They are here for us.

My mother, Janice, was a beautiful soul who sadly passed many years ago now after being diagnosed with ovarian cancer. Although we understood her condition at the time to be terminal, we were not sure exactly how long she would have to live.

I had never asked Emanuel for any guidance on my mother's condition, or any other health-related questions before this moment. I believe we should not delve into such things. But as the time grew nearer and I could see that she was in so much pain, I really wanted to know what her future would hold. In a way, it was a calling of my own desperation and the fear of loss I was facing.

I had returned home from work; it was the end of a busy week, and I was thankful it was Friday. My mother had been in my thoughts all day, and I was looking for some solace.

The house was quiet as no one else was home. I headed upstairs to sit on my bed, happy to sit in the stillness for a moment, surrounded by silence.

I kept my journal in my bedside drawer, and so I reached for it and a pen. I remember lighting a little candle and saying an opening prayer as I wrote the words ...

Dear Emanuel,

Please may I ask for your guidance around my mother, please? I cannot bear to see her suffering.

All will be well, child,

For it is the will of God, that she must be taken,

for her path was chosen long ago.

Now is the time for her to reach for her goals and go onto a greater good.

It is her learning, her being an angel of heart to be strong and faithful to God.

And we are all waiting with the grace of God

to be strong for her in this time of need.

We are waiting.

In the next few days to follow,

upon a new moon,

a time I cannot tell,

but she a willing soul to travel home with grace and beyond.

– My journal, dated 07/01/2010

I took a few moments to digest the information I had been given. I dried my tears, blew out the candle, and gave thanks for the message.

I was engulfed by a strange feeling, almost an inner numbness as a way of hiding my sadness.

I had been invited to my friend's house for dinner later on that evening – my beautiful and spiritual friend Helena, who has supported me in my own life's journey in many ways. I was so grateful to be going there, as it was always so welcoming.

During the dinner, I shared that I had asked Emanuel to help me with a writing session just before I had gone round to her house. This was not an unusual conversation for us to have, as we regularly shared our spiritual experiences over a glass of wine or two. It is always nice to have someone to share these experiences with who does not judge you and believes in Spirit. I went on to explain in detail that I had been feeling so overwhelmed with sadness the past few days, all surrounding my mother's condition. I felt that I really needed to have some clearer insight on the situation, even though my heart was already telling me what the outcome was to be, and I still needed to asked Emanuel for his guidance.

On reflection here, and re-reading the passage, I can clearly see that Emanuel was telling me my mother was ready to go and would pass in the days to follow around the next new moon.

As Helena and I read over the words again, we were both saddened by the passage. But in knowing that truth could have been given, we accepted the possibility that it could be so.

Helena suggested that we find out when the next new moon was to be, and so we referred to the internet for research on the topic. To our surprise, this was to be on Monday, the 10th of January, which in fact was only three days away. I remember the colour draining from my face as I registered this information. My thoughts were racing around my mind with endless disbelief. Surely, she still had longer than three days to live. I spent the rest of the evening trying to talk myself out of believing in the writing, saying to myself that maybe I had got it wrong or maybe I wasn't in the right frame of mind to be writing with Spirit at this time.

But, sure enough and true to Emanuel's words, my mother passed on Monday the 10th of January, the next new moon.

In the days that followed, I returned to my journal and thanked Emanuel for his honesty, and this is what he shared:

I am sorry for your loss.

Your mothers' bodily pain is to be no more, child,

For all is to be well now within her heart and in yours.

Janice is to grow now beyond others.

We will watch her well and develop her potential,

for she is here now to help others as I do.

Do not be sad, child, for it is God's will.

She is at peace, and so your heart will be

until you meet again

with love and grace.

Strange as it seems, these words actually make me smile now, as my grief has turned to understanding – the full and appreciative understanding that life goes on.

Writing these words with Emanuel has helped me to trust in the threads of life that we are all entwined by and unfold this beautiful gift of connection. Understand now that we do go on to live and re-live again and again. Accepting the process of our life's journey has led me onto future steps of my own. The universe is a big place, and we shall all have a space within it.

I have recently stepped out of my spiritual comfort zone to be seen. Whilst working on this book, I have accepted who I am, as Emanuel asks.

I have taken my own first steps to host a Spiritual Church service and deliver the Platform demonstration, with much encouragement from my mentors.

I have offered one-to-one spiritual guidance sessions through mediumship and helped to heal the hearts of many with words from Spirit.

But most importantly, I have learned to chart your soul plan.

I was drawn to the teachings of Blue Marsden and his soul plan reading techniques. I was led to book a course to learn this skill; my teacher was also named Jacqueline – the synchronicity of this made me laugh.

Looking into the power of your name and the energy that its behind it is very powerful. It leads us to a greater understanding of who we are and who we are here to be. It helps us to understand ourselves at a deeper level which brings us more clarity and understanding for who we are and the experiences we encounter in this lifetime we are living.

We all go through stages in our lives when we question who we are, or what we are doing here.

I have journeyed on this merry go round many, many times, still looking for the answers and not quite knowing which way to turn.

Loss has been a significant trigger in my own journey, as I have shared with you.

If you are feeling this calling, if you feel like you are searching, or you have a knowing that there is something more out there, then I say to you:

If you are ready to make peace with your challenges,

to identify your strengths and shine your light on your life's purpose, then you are ready for this profound healing and transformation to take place in your life,

and I welcome you to do so.

Emanuel, would you like to share the final words for Blessed Be?

There is never an ending, only a beginning, new beginnings.

I am ready.

You are ready.

The world is ready.

We are going to make a change.

We are changing and touching the hearts of many.

For those who are reading this book

who have lost a loved one,

or have lost themselves,

we are re-creating the purpose behind your daily lives.

We are daring to open your minds to the possibilities of a higher truth,

the possibilities that once you pass across the veil

that your spiritual life begins and can begin with a purpose.

You never truly die.

It is only your earthly body that may be forgotten.

We are soaring high through the cosmos,

fully bound, full of positive energy and light.

We are realigned to our souls' purpose,

and we learn from our path.

We learn from our journey,

and we then set out again for a new experience on the Earth,

as birth and rebirth.

You may live may lifetimes on the Earth plane,

for it is up to you how you live your journey.

May it be in peace, love and integrity.

Only you hold the key to unlock your heart,

to open and welcome the endless spiritual truths that await you.

Be free, be happy.

Live your life on the Earth through expression and experience.

Fill your hearts with joy.

Welcome this new existence into your time with hope.

There is a hope for a newer and better future on your Earth-bound plane

for all of you to share.

We will be by your side to help you to embrace these winds of change and allow the flow of continuity to sweep around you and through you without haste.

Allow it to be so.

And so, it will be.

As I am guiding Jacqueline, each of you have a guide with you.

Take this moment to thank them,

to greet them,

and welcome them into your journey,

for we cannot help you if we are not invited to do so.

Go within your heart space and feel the connection to the greater being that is you

and return to your source,

your gift of infinite love,

and share it will everyone you meet.

Until we meet again,

Amen Emanuel x

We are soaring high through the cosmos,

fully bound, full of positive energy and
light.

We are realigned to our souls' purpose, and
we learn from our path.

We learn from our journey,

and we then set out again for a new
experience on the

Earth, as birth and rebirth.

Final Word From Me

Well, what a journey that was.

When I started out with the intention of writing this book, I thought I would be writing a manual of step-by-step instructions for journaling with your angels and spirit guides.

Oh, how wrong I was.

With each chapter, I was taken on personal journey of trust, faith and self-belief. The unfolding of the story from the start of the book encouraged my curiosity like never before. Being led by Emanuel to delve deeper into the layers of time, I allowed the beauty of wisdom to unfold.

As a result of reading this book, I hope that you will now follow your own calling. I hope you will trust your inner voice and inner knowing to pull you in the direction of infinite possibilities and discovering what you are truly capable of.

My parting wish for you is this:

Allow your spirit guides to lead you forward.

Peel off the layers of doubt and step freely onto your path.

You are entering a new level of your spiritual growth and you are ready.

As you welcome and work with your guides, they will help you to align with your highest purpose and allow you to become the person you are truly here to be.

Feel the changes surround you.

You are already in a high vibration of love and positivity.

Know it.

Trust it.

Allow it.

You are ... it.

Until then, sparkle with Spirit.

Jac xx

P.S I can't wait to hear all of your stories. Please share them with me on my social media profiles.

Acknowledgements

I would like to thank Sean Patrick from That Guy's House for helping and trusting me, whilst bringing this book to life. He showed great patience and understanding, especially when I had a few wobble moments, where I nearly cancelled writing the whole thing. Thank you for encouraging me to block out the ego, face the fear and do it anyway :) You're the best!

To the team at That Guy's House who have worked on the project – Jesse Lynn Smart, Lynda Mangoro and Sarah Lloyd for contributing their amazing talents.

To my husband for believing in me, encouraging me to write this book and for being my constant throughout our rollercoaster of life experiences.

To my friends and soul sisters who listened and have been there throughout this journey.

To my children Katie, Euan & Eva for choosing me to be their mum.

Thank you to Muriel Murray, my first spiritual teacher, who showed me great patience and believed in me right from the very first circle session.

To Wendy Wharton my more recent spiritual mentor, who has helped me greatly in confidence and has guided me from being her student, onto participating in platform demonstrations.

To my amazing business coach Senga Cree for her constant ray of positivity. I thank you for your introduction to the fabulous Sharyn Anne McNeil, who shared my own soul destiny reading with me, which in turn changed my life!!

And to all my clients over the years who have supported me in many ways. And to those more recently who have invited me to host a reading session for them, both in person or by zoom, I thank you for being so open hearted and open minded, its been a honour delivering messages from your loved ones in spirit.

And finally to YOU, dear reader, thank you for buying this book and reading the words shared from Emanuel & me, it means the world to me.

If you feel so called, please connect with me on Instagram: _jacturner

About the Author

Jacqueline is a spiritual medium and lightworker, whose journey began as a beauty therapist. This later led her onto the path of a lightworker as she connected with other therapists and trained as a practitioner for Angel Healing, Crystal Healing and Reiki Master.

Since developing her skills as a medium through her local spiritualist centre, she has gone onto help hundreds of people to connect with their loved ones in spirit through her one-to-one reading sessions.

Interestingly, Jacqueline has a set of tarot cards which were gifted to her mother 27 years ago by a gypsy after a reading session. The gypsy insisted that her mother take them home to her daughter, who would be needing them in the future.

In addition to demonstrating mediumship, Jacqueline specialises as a Soul Plan practitioner, which can help to set about powerful healing and transformations within our lives. She hosts regular workshops and coaching sessions on the subject.

Emanuel & Me is Jacqueline's first book, published by That Guy's House. Her love of spiritual connection is reflected in the title of the book with the focus being on Emanuel, which means 'God is with us.'

Jacqueline, who is originally from Glasgow, now lives in the Northeast of Scotland, with her husband and three children.

Lightning Source UK Ltd.
Milton Keynes UK
UKHW022316290722
406581UK00006B/1076

9 781914 447419